GRETCHEN'S GOLD

THE STORY OF GRETCHEN FRASER:
AMERICA'S FIRST GOLD MEDALIST IN OLYMPIC SKIING

Carrying The Torch Beyond The Olympic Village

LIBRARY OF CONGRESS CATALOG CARD NO.
96-69802

ISBN 1-57510-019-3

FIRST PRINTING: October 1996

COVER ART BY
Bobbie Burns, Sun Valley, Idaho

BOOK DESIGN AND TYPOGRAPHY BY
Arrow Graphics, Missoula, Montana

PUBLISHED BY
Pictorial Histories Publishing Company, Inc.
713 South Third Street West, Missoula, Montana 59801

GRETCHEN'S GOLD

THE STORY OF GRETCHEN FRASER:
AMERICA'S FIRST GOLD MEDALIST IN OLYLMPIC SKIING

BY Luanne Pfeifer

Carrying the Torch Beyond The Olympic Village

PICTORIAL HISTORIES PUBLISHING COMPANY, INC.
Missoula, Montana

To those who carry the torch
beyond the Olympic Village.

TABLE OF CONTENTS

Bill Janss, Sun Valley, Idaho.

FOREWORD

AH, THE LATE 30S AND EARLY 40S, those were the days. We hiked up the mountains—skis slung over our shoulders—and then skied down as fast as our legs and equipment would carry us. Today when I ski Warm Springs run at Sun Valley via a high speed quad I wonder how I did it—both the long trek up and the quick descent down—all with those clumsy wooden skis and soft leather boots.

Ski racing sure has changed since I was selected as an alternate to the ill-fated 1940 Olympic Games which were cancelled while the world waged war. New wars have been fought and new ski areas have been built, but Sun Valley's Warm Springs run remains the same: still demanding, though a little wider with age. It remains the non-stop challenge it has always been.

I never thought then I would own (from 1964–1977) the resort I was training on. I never thought then that I would enjoy skiing the mountain as much, more than 55 years later, as I did then. But I do.

Another thing that endures constant is the large group of friends I've made on the ski slopes of Sun Valley through the years. Gretchen Fraser, especially, was one of them. Everyone who knew her was touched by her golden charm. Gretchen was always there to inspire everyone she met to forget their troubles, to enjoy life and to strive for excellence. I am glad her story is finally told in this book. Sun Valley will always be glamourous and touched with gold, in large part, because of her.

BILL JANSS
Sun Valley, 1996

Gretchen Fraser, 1919–1994

PREFACE

THERE IS A SAYING: "Courage is not always woven from the fabric that ostentation wears." I would never characterize Gretchen Fraser as ostentatious. But everybody who really knew her would label her as courageous. Thus the quotation proves to be very apropos for the principal subject of this book, Olympian Gretchen Fraser.

I had heard of Gretchen almost as soon as I started skiing in 1949, but did not meet her on a one-to-one basis until 1969 when she helped me in the early years of my journalistic career. We became friends—a friendship that started based on my professional ski writing career.

Later, when I purchased, in 1984, a small condo at Sun Valley to which I often fled, we became better friends. We met frequently in the social life of Sun Valley happenings where we shared some good thoughts—and some good laughs. I respected her, but I never knew what she thought of me.

Then one day, I walked into the remodeled Sun Valley Lodge and immediately spotted from the lobby straight through the open door of Gretchen's Restaurant something familiar. It was an article I had written in 1984 about her, matted, framed under glass and hung on the wall of her namesake restaurant in the famous lodge. I realized she honored me, or at least my words that I had written about her. So we became closer friends through the ensuing 10 years of her life.

Eight days after her death in 1994, while driving home to Malibu after attending her moving memorial service in the Sun Valley Lodge, I resolved to write her story.

There were many obstacles. More numerous, however, than all the obstacles were the people who helped me, acknowledged in the back of this book.

It was my primary concern in the recording of the events and facts of her life to get them correct in the historical context of when, where and how they happened. My personal perspective of why some things occurred is given in a parentheses aside just after some of the paragraphs written about the event. It is done this way, so as to not interrupt the flow of bringing the events to life. The Notes by Chapters in the back of the book further detail sources and things that may be of side interest to readers. They certainly interested me.

I was given the use of over 25 scrap books of hers filled with thousands of clippings of her life. Weeks of my life were spent extracting from them. The diary she kept for the Olympics and letters she wrote were also made available to me. Two years after Gretchen's and Don's deaths, their son, Bill, invited me into their home on Elkhorn Road, to spend the morning with him, remembering. He too gave me personal letters, and framed personal photos to add to the mounting avalanche of research I had accumulated by then.

I missed a lot of good ski days on Baldy (and summertime bike rides to Galena) sequestered in a room listening to Gretchen's and Don's oral history tapes, thoughtfully made, when Gretchen was alive. (Thank goodness Sun Valley values its place in ski history.) Along with newspaper clippings, I now had direct quotes from her, uttered at the time events occurred.

Yet there seemed, to me, to be few aspiring ski racers who knew anything of how America acquired its first alpine Olympic ski medals or the person who won them. It had been almost 50 years since Gretchen's gold in the Winter Olympics of 1948, yet no book had ever been done of her.

Thus, this book entered the start gate.

It was not written as simply a "how to" story on winning Olympic gold. I wanted readers to go beyond to get a sense of what one person did with her life after the Olympic applause died down.

Besides the gold and the silver of Olympic medals that Gretchen had won, there are many stories of gold jewelry pieces in this book—jewelry given to Gretchen and jewelry she gave to racers she admired. There are accounts of silver pieces, too—the silver belt buckle won in a pre-war race and silver candle sticks presented by a city in tribute to her after the Olympics. Scattered on the pages of this book are even tales of sapphires and diamonds.

I hope this book explains Averell Harriman's great desire to help the ski racers of America. The Tiffany gold pin that appears in text and photos several places in this book was simply the way of a very wealthy man to wish good luck to a promising racer—a racer who skied for the resort that he founded.

I hope this book also explains the unique love story of Don and Gretchen that no one can deny. To tell of Gretchen without including Don would be to tell only half the story. Most of all I hope the life of the person who attained America's first gold Olympic medal in skiing—and the gold medal performance in life that she led after the Olympics—will live on in the lives of anyone who has the courage to dream the impossible dream.

If there's one thing I learned from writing this book it is that Gretchen never gave up—even when the war cancelled the first Olympics to which she had been chosen … even when she was thought too old to try out for the Olympic ski team … even when the world press said that none of the American women had a chance in the '48 Winter Olympics in St. Moritz, Switzerland.

Likewise after the Olympics she never wavered from the causes to which she aspired. Even when she didn't have any

xi

idea how to teach the war amputees to ski, she did get them to ski. Even when she faced mounting medical problems of her own, she, without a complaint, kept up an active life. The bottom line is: She always found a way to do all the "impossible" things that she did. She never gave up.

LUANNE PFEIFER
Malibu, California

INTRODUCTION

FEBRUARY, 1994

It was snowing lightly in one of those silent Sawtooth
snowfalls. All through the night the flakes fell vertically, not in
the horizontal slashings of so many February storms. In the
morning when the Wood River Valley awoke, everything was
freshly painted white and skiers rejoiced since for weeks there
had been no new snow, except for what the amazingly adequate
snow making machines spewed on the ski runs.

Softly it continued: the overnight miracle of whitewashing
the roads, the pathways, the rail fence tops, and the roof tops
with the fresh scrubbed look. Brightly clad excited visitors to
Sun Valley were collecting at the circle next to the famed Lodge
just as skiers had since the resort began in 1936. It had been 58
years since they first gathered here for the buses to take them
to ski the surrounding famed mountains of southern Idaho.

Excitement ran high with the jubilant proclamations of
"powder," but then someone noticed the flag on the village
flagpole was flying at half-mast. First one person boarding the
Warm Springs bus commented on it, a second person, and then
many. No one knew why.

That day softly and slowly, all over the mountain, the message that Gretchen Fraser had died began to spread. To a few
cognoscenti it was as if she had directed the night of the silent
snow. Even Hollywood couldn't have produced a better ending. For the snow that fell so beautifully on the trees, parkas
and eyelashes seemed to be her last and parting present to skiers at the resort in the West where she had lived a good part of

her life. How typical of Gretchen to leave a treasured gift.

She had been fighting cancer and heart problems for years, yet in the end it was her heart that gave out. America had lost the first person to wrest from European domination, an Olympic gold medal in skiing. Sun Valley was now bereft of a living treasured icon. Even before the finish line of her 75 years of life she had become a legend, without fanfare and trumpets, of ski racing in the United States.

FEBRUARY, 1948

"ST. MORITZ (AP)—In a surprise upset a pigtailed western American housewife named Gretchen Fraser, 28, who trained at Sun Valley, Idaho racked up a gold in the Special Slalom of the Vth Winter Olympic Games. . . ."

When those words were cabled from Switzerland around the world few people knew of the ski resort in the Sawtooth Mountains of Idaho somewhere in the American West. Even fewer knew of her.

A decade earlier international ski racing in the United States had a dazzling start, but was soon interrupted by war. In 1948 when the first post war Olympic Games were held, America acquired an international hero—one destined for role model status.

The torch was lit and she became a long-time keeper of the flame. Yet with the passing of years even people who frequently ski her namesake run called Gretchen's Gold, high on Seattle Ridge at the resort of Sun Valley, know much about her or other early trend setters of the sport. It was another era. The snows, huzzahs and heroes of a dozen winter Olympic games have subsequently muted that record.

This story, "Gretchen's Gold," starts early in the century when the ski sport was young in the United States and so was she. . . .

ONE

Paradise

I̅N A WAY, America's path to Olympic ski greatness can be said to start back in Norway, the country that gave birth to skiing as a sport. For the woman destined to win America's first alpine Olympic medals had a mother, Clara Andersen Kunigk, who was from Tonsberg, Norway. As a resident of Scandinavia's oldest town, Clara passed on the legacy of her homeland to her children, even when she was later far away and living in the Pacific Northwest part of the United States.

Married to a German immigrant, Willibald Alphons Kunigk, Clara gave birth to two children. The first was a boy who was named William. The second child, a girl, she named Gretchen, a Scandinavian derivative of Margaret meaning the pearl. There were bright hopes that February 11, 1919, when her only daughter was born. The armistice of World War I had been signed three months previously and optimism ran high throughout the land.

The Kunigks were living in Tacoma, Washington. There Willibald, a German immigrant and self-taught engineer, was the longtime head of the city's water utility, eventually to become known as "the father of Tacoma's water supply." He was the re-cipient of a national award for distinguished service in the water supply field. After serving the water utility for 39 years he retired.

Tonsberg, Norway, home of Gretchen's mother.   ALLISON RAAUM

The Kunigk's son, Bill, was born while America was still at war but their daughter, Gretchen Claudia, was born a year and a half later, in peace. It was a good omen.

While growing up in Tonsberg, Clara had learned to ski and she loved it. Nearby was a skiing track of 3 km (1.8 miles) to Strengsdal Lake. This was supplemented by a 150 meter (485 foot) vertical downhill slope.

So it was natural that Clara give her American-born children skis for Christmas. It was a time when America was just learning about the sport and a mother, let alone a woman, who skied was a rarity. It was 1932 when Gretchen, 13 years old, received her first pair of skis. Her brother, almost two years older, also received skis at that same time.

Clara Kunigk took them both off on their first ski trip, to Paradise Inn at Mount Rainier's Paradise Valley. The mountain is

Clara Kunigk with her children Bill and Gretchen.

a 14,410 foot high volcanic peak with 26 glaciers, about 60 miles southeast of the two cities of Seattle and Tacoma. On the days when it is visible from these cities it dominates the Cascade range and few people on the urban streets fail to comment on its grandeur. The Indians long ago worshipped it.

The National Park Service maintained a lodge at Paradise Valley. Anyone from Seattle or Tacoma with any inkling of the sport in the 30s would congregate here but, as big brother

LEFT: *Gretchen and Bill with their mother on Mount Rainier.*
RIGHT: *Gretchen in riding breeches with her first skis.*

Bill Kunigk remembers, "It was a big day when there were a dozen skis leaning against the inn."

Skiers entered on the south side of Rainier, drove by beautiful Longmire, the snout of Nisqually glacier, then on to Narada Falls. The road was usually not plowed past Narada Falls so skiers often parked their cars here, hoisted their skis on their shoulders, and tramped about 1½ miles up the ever-steepening road to finally enter Paradise.

By the time Bill got his driver's license (1935) brother and sister still strapped sealskins to the bottoms of their skis to aid in the climbs for the skiing above Paradise Inn. Not until 1937 was a rope tow installed at Paradise. Gretchen and her brother had spent their earliest ski days hiking up to ski down.

Little by little Rainier became the focus of Pacific Northwest racing. Under the auspices of the National Park Service instructors were hired to run an embryo ski school. Once Gretchen had learned to ski a bit from her mother, she wanted to enter some of the weekend novice races open to anyone.

The racing tradition on Mount Rainier was started in 1934 when Hans Otto Giese talked a bunch of sturdy young men in knickers to enter the first Silver Skis Championships. Giese was a local skiing pioneer who suggested the race to boost the region and the infant sport of downhill racing. It was a ski racing spectacular sponsored by the Seattle newspaper, the *Post Intelligencer.*

At the sound of a shotgun, 60 skiers all at once started poling and plunging, falling and flying on skis down from Camp Muir at Rainier's 10,000 foot level to Paradise Inn more than 4,500 feet and four miles below. They were all members of local clubs (Seattle Mountaineers, Seattle Ski Club, Paradise Ski Club and Washington Ski Club) trying to prove to the world that the Northwest offered unparalleled skiing if not spectacular skiers.

In 1934 there was no such thing as snow grooming. From the *geschmozzle* (simultaneous) start, on the edge of Cowlitz Glacier the course plunged down the rolling washboard of Muir Snowfield, past McClure Rock, down to Panorama Point (where there was a traffic jam of fallen bodies) and across Skyline Trail. The course flattened out below Alta Vista at elevation 5,940 feet and the racers then had to pole to the finish at Paradise Inn.

Just a few hundred yards after the start, the racers were funneled into a chute for the first of only two gates. Most racers were out of control. It was like hitting a washboard at 50 mph, some competitors later recalled. Moreover, even before they started the brutal race that morning they had to climb for 2½ to 3 hours to the start at Camp Muir. They also had to deal with the problem of waxing wooden skis for conditions that ranged from ice to slush. Temperatures varied from 26 degrees at Muir to 46 degrees at Paradise.

P-I file/1934

Hans Otto Giese, Don Fraser and Alf Moystad (left to right) pose after the 1934 Silver Skis Championship on Mount Rainier. Giese is credited with coming up with the race idea as a way to give the budding sport of downhill skiing a local boost.

SILVER METTLE

Hell-bent memories still fresh after 60 years

The "Silver Skis" Championship is remembered 60 years later.

A typical reporter's view of the race wrote it as five miles in length with a drop of 5,000 feet, another reported it 3.9 miles and a 4,600 foot vertical drop. Obviously there were no press releases as there are today to aid in ski race coverage.

Ben Thompson founder of Anderson & Thompson Skis broke his jaw in that first Rainier race. That was the only serious accident until 1940, when Sig Hall was killed after crashing into rocks.

An undergraduate from University of Washington, Don Fraser, won that first Silver Skis Championship finishing in 10 minutes 49.6 seconds, surviving the ski-tangled starts and high speed melee which followed. Attending University of Washington during the day and working at Boeing Aircraft Company he still had time to make his own wooden skis of birch and poles out of bamboo. A friend improvised to make his then "high tech" boots.

Giese's Silver Skis race did have the desired effect of boosting racing for the growing sport of skiing. The following winter after that initial Silver Skis race, America picked its first ever alpine Olympic ski team. The tryouts were held on Mount Rainier as part of the first U.S. National Alpine Combined Championships.

Hannes Schroll from Bischofshoven, Austria, yodeling most of the way down the courses, took first in the slalom and downhill. The racers seemed to be having the most fun on the mountains. It was all taken in by a teenage girl named Gretchen Kunigk dressed in riding breeches, watching in awe from the sidelines.

Don Fraser was selected for the 1936 Winter Olympics on the merits of his 1934 Silver Skis win and the 1935 Rainier National Championships. He received a letter of his selection to the team stating he would receive $75 plus free room and board once at the Olympic site in Garmish-Partenkirchen, Germany. Travel expenses would be his own responsibility. So he worked his way abroad on a Norwegian freighter, chipping rust and painting the decks.

Don Fraser in Canada, circa late 1930s.

"It took 31 days at pay of $1/day. Being selected to the Olympic team meant I received a $50 overcoat, plus cap, hat and sweater," documented Don.[1]

He landed in Le Havre and took a train to Garmisch-Partenkirchen for the IVth Winter Olympic Games. Once there he had two weeks free room and board. As fate would have it

Don Fraser (right) and 1936 Olympic cross country coach Sven Utterstrom standing in front of the Post Hotel Nebenhaus (annex).

Don hit a tree in practice, injured his hip and did not race.

Best U.S. finisher, Dick Durrance, placed eighth in the slalom and 11th in downhill for a 10th in the combined. Twenty-two men had been selected for the U.S. 1936 Olympic ski team. They were divided into alpine, cross country and jumping competitors. (In this first Olympics to include alpine events, medals were awarded only for alpine combined results.)

For the women, thirteen counting the alternates were named to the first Women's Olympic ski team. Three were injured before the Games and only four allowed to race. All were alpine ski racers but no uniforms were made, so they wore red stockings and knickers to distinguish themselves as a team. They caused no ripples in racing circles but they did get high marks as a fashion statement.

German chancellor Adolf Hitler, from a balcony high above the athletes, opened the IV Winter Olympics for over 1000 competitors from 28 nations on February 2, 1936.

Don later told of how the American team's uniforms and equipment received quite a bit of scrutiny from the Nazi contingent when they walked around the Olympic village. Swastikas were in abundance but few Americans recognized then the smolderings of a world war that was to erupt before the nations of the world could come together for the next scheduled Olympic Games.

After the Games most of the same American team went to the Fédération International de Ski (FIS) races in Innsbruck, Austria held the next month where records state it was 15 degrees above zero and the course was a sheet of ice. A bulletin of the men's downhill read: six broken legs, two fractured collar bones, 21 DNF (did not finish) out of 57 racers. For the women, though none was injured, only about half completed the course which was shortened, after protests by U.S. women's team manager, Alice Damrosch Wolfe (Kiaer), by 500 yards. Such was the state of ski racing in those days.

The highest placing Americans at those post-Olympic FIS races were Dick Durrance with 11th in the combined and Betty Woolsey with a 10th in the women's downhill.

(After World War II the FIS World Ski Championships were not held in an Olympic year. It was a good decision. Merely from my journalist's point of view alone, the media hype for two such events, held in the same year, could dilute the importance of each event.)

After the FIS Don went on to compete in the Marmolata Downhill in Marmolata, Italy and the Kings Cup (six downhill races in six consecutive days) in Sestriere, Italy.

When the races were over, many of the athletes including Don, embarked on a 3,000-mile bicycle ride starting in Munich and pedaling through Germany, Switzerland, and the Netherlands.

Meanwhile back in America the bright spot overshadowing America's first alpine skiing foray into Olympic competition was that before the year ran out, the ski resort of Sun Valley opened in the state of Idaho. While *Life* Magazine focused on the movie stars and Social Register Eastern society who flocked to the resort, a quiet revolution in America's ski racing was brewing, much to the credit of Sun Valley's founder, W. Averell Harriman.

Harriman, while chairman of the board of the Union Pacific Railroad, hired in 1936 an Austrian count, Felix Schaffgotsch, to search America's western mountains for a place to build a destination ski resort. Well traveled, sports minded and born to wealth, Harriman had seen the popular European ski resorts of the Alps and once lamented, "If they can have it, why can't I?"

His motive was not only personal. The Union Pacific Railroad needed something to attract passenger travel from the East to the American West to bring in added revenue. So the count was kept from wandering too far from the umbilical cord of the railroad and always had U.P. officials to shepherd him.

When the search seemed dead-ended after roaming California, Oregon, Utah, Wyoming and Colorado, the count came under the reluctant chaperonage of the Union Pacific's man in Boise, William J. Hynes. Hynes showed him most of Idaho forgetting about the Ketchum-Hailey area bordering the Sawtooth Mountains. The count left Idaho and only then did Hynes remember that the company's most expensive branch line to keep open in winter lead to a beautiful valley. The line was sporadically in service to serve as a sheep shipping spur for a pot-bellied stove-heated train that twice a week puffed up from Shoshone to Ketchum, where ever that was.

Hynes had to call Count Schaffgotsch back by telegram. The count returned to Idaho even though the train wasn't running. The weather too, didn't permit the entry by road from Shoshone to Ketchum in January but Hynes, the count, and District Engineer Matt Johnson, promptly chartered a bus. They got stuck in the ever-deepening snow at Timmerman Hill and a snowplow on reconnaissance from Shoshone finally led the unlikely parade past Bellevue, past Hailey and on into Ketchum.

Ketchum: population 270. Make that about 135 in the dead of winter on January, 19, 1936 when the count arrived.

The day after they arrived the sun was out, the air was dry, and all the mountains surrounding the valley were resplendent in the new fallen snow. In an expansive meadow a mile from town the count noticed that none of the mountains cast their shadow on the large windless valley. He wired Harriman that he found what he was looking for.

Schaffgotsch did not discover the valley lodge site all by himself. He was told that it ought to be where the stock cattle of the Brass Ranch always congregated to take in the warm air currents. It was the final climax to days of trekking the surrounding mountains, for then he knew he had found the place to build Harriman's luxury mountain lodge which became the focal point of the first newly created, dedicated, destination ski resort in America.

Even to this day when visitors to Sun Valley drive out of Ketchum along the Sun Valley Road for a mile the same feeling of a-prelude-to-grandeur takes place. In the vernacular of today it's called "good vibes." The entrance road to Sun Valley village, especially when the rail fence is draped with new snow or strung with Christmas lights in modern times, seldom fails to evoke the same pangs of enchantment as it did for its discoverer back in 1936.

The ground was broken in May for the mountain lodge and by December 21, 1936, it was finished and a grand opening staged. It was built to be magnificent in every way: outdoor heated swimming pool, indoor luxurious dining tables draped in pale yellow against the backdrop of white mountains everywhere. A ski school with five instructors under the direction of Hans Hauser, three time Austrian champion, awaited guests.

On Harriman's orders a Union Pacific engineer named Jim Curran was asked to invent an indulgent way of getting guests on skis up the mountains. The embryo lifts were put up on Proctor and Dollar mountains. Curran connived a kind of conveyor system patterned after davit-and-hook devices which loaded bananas on fruit boats in South America for the company he worked for before joining Union Pacific. The difference in Curran's device was that the hooks were replaced by chairs for skiers to sit down. Thus evolved the world's first chairlift.

(The Proctor chairlift was later moved to Ruud Mountain, where the towers remain in modern times as silent relics of the past.)

Another thing Harriman wanted for his ski resort was an international ski race where Americans could test themselves against the world's best. "In Europe the Kandahar race was well known so it was my idea to start a ski race similar to it because we were so far behind Europeans in ski competition," he said.[2] It was first called the Sun Valley International but the name soon was changed, by the racers, to The Harriman Cup.

On March 12 and 13, 1937, top European ski racers, some of whom had been imported as ski instructors, competed against a growing group of American skiers from across the country. In an unexpected upset, Dick Durrance of Dartmouth College gained first place ahead of such international ski champions as Hans Hauser, then the Sun Valley Ski School head, who had won most of the important European races in former years.

Durrance had learned to ski in Germany where his mother with his brothers and sisters lived for six years from 1926 to 1933 while Dick was a teenager.

The first Harriman Cup was a rugged race in the still-undeveloped Boulder Mountains north of Sun Valley. After Durrance took 1st in the downhill, slalom and combined that initial race year, the summit was re-named Durrance Mountain.

(The peak where the racers climbed to the top, starting at dawn, is visible today on the right-hand side of Highway 75 about seven miles north out of Ketchum after passing Lake Creek. Look for the wide treeless bowl after passing the Sawtooth National Recreation Area headquarters building.)

While the first Harriman Cup was being staged, Gretchen Kunigk was in the Pacific Northwest going to high school and going skiing as often as possible. In the summer she rode horses and wished more than a few times to be a female jockey. She was the only 16-year-old girl jockey in the state of Washington at the state fair in Puyallup. Petite and athletic she made a good race horse rider.

Fate led her in another direction in 1936 when Otto Lang, of the Hannes Schneider ski school of St. Anton, Austria came to Mount Rainier to make a ski instruction movie with Jerome Hill of America's Great Northwest Pacific Railroad fortune. Lang was so enamored with Mount Rainier that he stayed to accept an invitation to open the West's first official Arlberg ski school at Paradise Inn in December, 1936. Ken Syverson who already worked there became his assistant.

Gretchen had been watching the top ranked racers on Rainier and wanted to enter the competitors' domain. As luck would have it, Lang arrived at the right time and was there to help. She had learned the rudiments of the sport from her mother and was now at a steady snow plow stage.

Don Fraser wins Silver Skis for a second time, 1938.

On the slopes of Rainier raw talent and grit were shaped into refined ability and steady proficiency by Lang. "In a very short time, I detected that this young lady had the determination and doggedness to go places . . . She grasped the important technical points very quickly and improved rapidly." related Lang.[3]

While the first Harriman Cup (1937) was being staged at Sun Valley, ski racing was also taking hold in the Northwest. The Spokane Ski Club had built a log cabin clubhouse in 1933 near the top of Mount Spokane. Races were held weekends on a downhill course set above the club's cabin ending with a straight slide down a small slalom hill next to the cabin.

In 1937 the Northwest Championships were held there and that is where Gretchen won her first big race, skiing for the Washington Ski Club of Seattle. The Spokane Ski Club advertised it would have five outdoor bonfires in addition to the club cabin to provide warmth for spectators who were advised to wear the warmest of clothing—"heavy stockings and shoes in particular."

Seven hundred cars showed up in the parking lot and the 1937 Northwest Championships were on. They watched Gretchen from Tacoma take a third in the downhill, a second in the slalom to win the combined title.

The racers Gretchen beat out of the combined title on the slopes of Mount Spokane were good, but not considered of consequence. Women were only starting to be recognized as international race competitors and thus none was invited to compete in the first Harriman Cup Race at Sun Valley.

Another racer traveling to Mount Spokane for the Pacific Northwest Championships that year was Don Fraser, who left shortly afterwards to travel to the first Harriman Cup race at Sun Valley where he placed 18th. Before leaving Mount Spokane, however, he won first in the combined. The two combined winners couldn't help but notice each other as they continued to gather successive trophies at race award ceremonies throughout the Pacific Northwest.

The Averell Harriman family on the ski slopes at Sun Valley, 1937. On the left, Mrs. Marie Harriman (former wife of Cornelius Vanderbilt Whitney); on the right, W. Averell Harriman. They flank Averell Harriman's two daughters, Kathleen and Mary. Kathleen is second from left. STEVE HANNIGAN PHOTO, 1969 PERSONAL COLLECTION W. AVERELL HARRIMAN, WASHINGTON, D.C.

There was a three-to-one ratio of men to women ski racers in the Pacific Northwest at that time with about 30 men entered in the competitions and about 10 to a dozen women always showing up.

After one race Gretchen invited Don to her house for a family celebration of her birthday. It was only then that the two racers discovered they shared the same birth date: February ll.

(Don was born February 11, 1913 and Gretchen February 11, 1919)

As the '37 ski season turned to spring skiing, to reward his prodigy for her racing progress, Otto Lang gave Gretchen a chance to ski in a big Hollywood movie as an action double for a new star, Sonja Henie.

The fabulous Sonja had recently been signed by Darryl Zanuck to a 20th Century Fox contract on the strength of deep dimples, lilting Norwegian accent and three Olympic women's figure skating gold medals. To pump up her second film for him with a bit of heroic action, Zanuck decided to throw in some exotic stuff—like skiing which now was enticing a steady stream of participants. Sonja, with help from a few stand-ins, proved she was not just a one-picture flash of winter lightning on the Silver Screen.

The studio sent a shooting script to Lang to solicit his help finding locations on Rainier. In March, Henie arrived, heading an entourage that included co-star Tyrone Power (a new and rising face in Hollywood), director David Butler and a camera crew who were challenged to shoot ski footage climaxing in a big drop off a cornice.

After seeing Sonja ski, Lang realized she'd need a double. He picked his racer, Gretchen, who had Henie's build and body type, as a double for the female lead in one of the first Hollywood films ever to dramatically incorporate skiing scenes. Title: "Thin Ice."

For 20 consecutive days the weather closed in and the cameras stopped rolling. Sonja and Tyrone were obviously getting better acquainted in their private quarters at Paradise Inn. The studio grew tired of paying high-priced talent for what had become a romantic tryst on some far flung mountain top—with no film footage resulting.

So the studio ordered its stars back to Hollywood, while Butler left Lang in charge of the ski camera crew. Darryl F. Zanuck later remarked, Lang was remarkably adapt at film coverage. Gretchen handled her part creditably too, but she wasn't quite ready for the cornice jump, so Lang, wearing a blond wig squeezed into Henie's blouse (slit down the back) and did the cornice jump scene.

The film was a catalyst for the sport's ongoing romance with Hollywood that early in the game did so much to pro-

Sonja Henie, Tyrone Power and Gretchen during filming of "Thin Ice," 1937. A SNAPSHOT IN GRETCHEN'S SCRAPBOOK

mote the idea of skiing—something Americans were just beginning to embrace. *Variety* (a Hollywood publication which can make or break a movie production) rated "Thin Ice" a double A and proclaimed it "a box office winner" when it premiered in August, 1937.

As for Don Fraser, when the '37 winter waned in the West and summertime spread over the North American mountains, the Farellones of South America, as host resort, invited him to the Pan Am Games. It was then winter south of the equator.

The Ski Club of Chile invited the best ski racers of France, Austria, Germany, America, Argentina and Chile to compete in the Pan Am Championships of 1937. Don Fraser was invited for that summer conclave. To get there he went by boat for 33 days, then car and finally a donkey. Farellones is a ski resort about 60 miles east of Santiago, Chile. It was worth the long trip for he won the slalom and took second in the combined among the international ski set.

Count Felix Schaffgotsch (left) and Averell Harriman at the Lodge, Sun Valley, 1937. Note no trees around lodge. STEVE HANNEGAN AND ASSOC.

After the Championships Don joined a French-Italian climbing expedition to climb Mt. Tupungato (22,300 feet) on the Chile-Argentina border. He had climbed in the Cascades of North America so he took the opportunity to climb, in central and southern Chile, other peaks of lesser heights than Mt. Tupungato which is one of the five highest mountains in all of South America.

His scrap book of his South American adventure naturally displays photos of the Chilean mountains but also several pages are devoted to photos of freighters in boat harbors loading bananas on board. Don had remembered the Union Pacific railroad had used the South American banana-rigs as its inspiration for inventing the world's first chair lift.

During the next winter both Don and Gretchen kept meeting on award platforms for ski races in the Pacific Northwest. On February 14–15, 1938, a Winter Sports Carnival was held on Mount Rainier. It was a two day festival of racing, dancing and camaraderie at Paradise Valley. Winner of the women's open slalom was Gretchen Kunigk with Don Fraser taking the men's title. Ironically, Gretchen's prize was one week's free ski lessons.

The carnival culminated with a ball at Paradise Inn. Blonde-haired Gretchen was crowned queen and reigned over the festivities, flanked by two attendants, Shirley McDonald and Blanche Barre. The newspaper photographers were beginning to notice that glamour, at least on the distaff side, had entered the ski racing scene.

On Mount Hood in Oregon the season culminated with both Gretchen and Don winning the combined of the 1938 Pacific Northwest Championships there. Don's combined win was on the strength of a first place in the slalom. Gretchen's was based on the combination of a second in the slalom and a first in the downhill.

As a result both were invited to enter the 1938 Harriman Cup at Sun Valley on March 12 and 13, 1938. Fate inevitably linked them together forever on the mountains and inevitably to Sun Valley after that.

*Averell Harriman and Mrs. Marie Harriman at Sun Valley in the
1930s.* HARRIMAN COLLECTION

TWO

The Harriman Cup

THE SUMMER AFTER Sun Valley opened, Averell Harriman's publicity dynamo, Steve Hannegan, talked Paramount Pictures into filming at the resort the ski scenes of "I Met Him in Paris" starring Claudette Colbert. The Swiss village set, constructed in a nearby canyon, looked so at home in the Sawtooth mountains and so appropriate to house the young ski racing crowd for whom Harriman wanted affordable accommodations that its movie design found its way to the Union Pacific offices via the architectural firm of Gilbert Stanley Underwood of Los Angeles and Washington, D.C. (The same firm that had done the Lodge.) The railroad named the inn Challenger after one of its trains. (In 1972 the name was changed to Sun Valley Inn.)

The movie was the first—but not the last—time Hollywood was to leave its lasting imprint on Sun Valley.

Thus, the racers arriving for the second Harriman Cup at Sun Valley found new accommodations had been constructed. The Inn ($8/night), built in Swiss-Tyrolean style, was more economical than the luxurious Sun Valley Lodge ($24/night) so the former drew the college students and young ski racers. Later chalets were built in back of the inn where competitors could stay for $1/night, four to a room.

One of the competitors, Hannah Locke from the East Coast, invited by Harriman to train out West in Sun Valley, stayed in

Kathleen Harriman

one of these double-bunk chalet rooms. She had met many of the racers while skiing in Europe when she was on the first U.S. women's Olympic and FIS ski teams.

Years later, the same racer, now Mrs. Hannah Locke Carter, seated in her mansion in the exclusive Bel Air region of Los Angeles, related—incongruous to her present setting—how she slept in a bunk bed and shared a hallway-telephone where every-one heard the private conversations of others. As she was a Sun Valley racer-in-training she worked for the resort keeping records as secretary for the Sun Valley Ski Club and skied persistently, resulting in her being named to the 1940 U.S. Olympic alpine team. Originally she had aspirations to be a figure skater but one year skiing at Sun Valley changed it.

Another young racer who had come on his first visit to Sun Valley about this time was Bill Janss. He too stayed in one of the $1/night/person chalet rooms. Sun Valley's enchantment struck again—even from the confines of a quadruple-shared bunk room. His Janss Corporation became the resort's second owner in 1964.

The Inn was less stuffy than the opulent Lodge, just what the racers needed. They loved to dance schottisches, polkas and later the Hokey Pokey in the Ram of the Inn rather than to slow-sway to the Lodge's Duchin Room trio. One movie star, David Niven, also considered the Inn more fun than the Lodge.[1]

Sun Valley, at the time, was filled with movie stars, eastern socialites, top American business heads, and Greek shipping magnates, all under the tutelage of the original six Austrian ski instructors, supplemented by a few other foreigners and Americans. It was a United States winter utopia with a wooden-sidewalk town consisting mostly of bars and casinos in Ketchum (one mile away); pristine mountain scenery out every guest's window and two rather primitive but effective new-fangled chair lifts (one on Dollar Mt. and other on Proctor Mt.). Sleighs went around the pathways and on romantic moonlit treks to Trail Creek Cabin, an old hunting cabin, deep in the woods beyond the accommodations.

There was a two-to-one, employee-to-guest ratio. Every visitor was pampered. A half dozen lots around Sun Valley Lake were being sold for house building. The year before Harriman cottage, a modest five bedroom residence, was built close to the Lodge for Sun Valley's founder.

Sun Valley had not developed Bald Mountain when the second Harriman Cup races were held March 12, 1938. So the competitors again were up at dawn to catch the buses for the half hour ride and another long climb up newly named Durrance Mountain for the downhill. The only shelter at the top of the course was behind some rocks. A wet snow was falling.

"We were all drowned rats. Everyone appreciated the prompt warm transportation back to the Inn," described Gretchen about her first Harriman Cup race.[2] The women crouched on the mountainside, wet and miserable, waiting for their turn to race after all the men had completed the course. To add to their woes, the course was badly cut up by the time it was their turn to race.

(I often wonder how anyone thought of ski racing as fun in those days—without the high tech fabrics of the late 1990s, without lifts, without grooming, without shelter; but they did. From my own perspective years later when I started ski racing at Mammoth Mountain, California racing had improved little in creature comforts. The ruts were deep—sometimes so deep I could barely see out of them. The race results were written at a picnic table and I had only one mission if I ever won another race: I'd put portable Ladies Rooms at the top of every race course. Yet it was fun and the camaraderie of racers I met then endures in a special bonding aquired between all those who wait their turn to enter a start gate. It just lasts on . . . and on through the ages.)

For the 1938 Harriman Cup, Grace Carter Lindley who married Al Lindley, Sun Valley Ski Club president, having met him at the 1936 Olympics, swept the women's downhill and slalom capturing the combined. The men's portion was won again by Dick Durrance.

The skis which the Harriman racers coveted most were made by Attenhofer and by Groswold. They were on the order of 236 cm. long. Bindings carried the brand names: Huitfeldt, Alpine and

Kathleen Harriman digs out as Clarita Heath in ski skirt looks on.
Clarita was a 1936 Olympic ski team member. SUN VALLEY NEWS BUREAU

Kandahar. The Sun Valley Ski Club president called it the "Golden Age of Skiing" with the height of technology.[2]

There was a lot of action going on both on and off the race courses. Life-long liaisons were made here. Many competitors lost their hearts, heads and even some races at Sun Valley.

There were two racers from the Reno Ski Club at the '38 Harriman, who had life long marriages start in Sun Valley. The two racers were Wayne Poulsen and Marti Arrougé. The latter stayed on to become a ski instructor after the race.

Wayne went back to Reno to teach skiing at Mt. Rose, then enlisted in Royal Air Force (RAF). While waiting to be called he went back to Sun Valley to teach skiing.

Once there, Dorice Taylor of Sun Valley's publicity department introduced one of her former debutant students (Gladys "Sandy" Kunau) from fashionable Miss Hewitt's Girls' School in the East to Wayne Poulsen. At the time he was the private ski instructor for a Greek tycoon named Stavros Niarchos. Niarchos arrived at Sun Valley with a group of Greek compatriots from Chicago. Most of the days the Greek millionaire was so hung over from drinking and gambling that he kept calling to cancel his private lesson. Thus Poulsen's romance blossomed when Wayne found he had time to pursue Sandy.

The resulting marriage of Wayne and Sandy Poulsen produced eight Poulsen children, four of whom were on the United States national ski team with two of them (Sandra and Eric Poulsen) on the U.S. 1972 Olympic team. Wayne was the founding force behind Squaw Valley, California development. When he died in 1995 they had been married 53 years, always returning to Sun Valley for ski club reunion week of races, *gemutlichkeit* and dancing.

Arrouge's marriage to movie super star Norma Shearer was a love at first season romance. Coming to Sun Valley after the death of her husband, Irving Thalberg (vice president and supervisor of production for MGM movie studios), she fell in love with the Basque sheepherder's son from Reno. He was first hired to teach skiing to the Thalberg's son but then later instructed the mother. He lovingly took care of the movie star to her death which occurred after many years, suffering a severe form of memory loss.

Also falling under the spell of Sun Valley were Dick Durrance from Dartmouth College, in the East and Margaret (Miggs) Jennings from California in the West. The two racers were celebrating 55 years of marriage in 1995 and still going strong. While riding a chair lift at Aspen-Snowmass with me, in 1995, Miggs attributed the lasting effect of sharing so many outdoor recreational activities together, to the enduring marriages of the early racers.

Count Schaffgotsch (left) and Hans Hauser wax before a Harriman Cup race.

Into the list of lasting love affairs that happened about that time in Sun Valley fell the two Pacific Northwest ski racers, Gretchen Kunigk and Don Fraser. For the '38 Harriman Cup these racers took the train, Portland Rose, to Idaho from Seattle. Don, who had been to the first Harriman Cup the year before, delighted in showing the resort to Gretchen on her first trip there. They went together on the sleigh through the woods to Trail Creek Cabin for the pre-race competitors' dinner. Once at the cabin Averell Harriman, astute in such matters, could see the blossoming love affair between the two racers and took the opportunity to announce their engagement. Only trouble was Don had not proposed—yet.

"Marriage wasn't something I was thinking about then," said Don.

Don Fraser, captain of the Washington Ski Club, came in

An early-day sleigh like the one Don and Gretchen rode to Trail Creek Cabin at Sun Valley. SUN VALLEY CO.

ninth in the downhill, sixth in the slalom and sixth in the combined. On her first trip to Sun Valley Gretchen Kunigk came in third in the downhill, fourth in the slalom and took second in the combined.

Both left shortly after the 1938 Harriman Cup to compete in the Mount Rainier Silver Skis race where Don gained his second win in the legendary Washington race and Gretchen captured a first place with her first entry in the competition which she had watched from the sidelines four years before.

Skiing was still going strong at Mount Hood in June where the Golden Rose race was held late in the season. To the tune of a terrific thunderstorm the race wound up with a finish gate just east of Timberline Lodge, which had been open less than a year. Fred McNeil was an official that day at the finish and had insisted that, because of the crowd, the gate was too narrow, also should be better marked. So it was widened. Even so, Gretchen, who came down at a terrifying clip, crashed into the gate. Nevertheless she got through as she fell. Though she won the race she was able to walk only a few feet away before collapsing. The result: torn ligaments in her knee and torn leg cartilages which kept her out of competition for most of the next ski season (the winter of '38–39).

It was not until the end of the season in April 1939 when the Northwest Ski Championships were held that she returned to competition. She missed the first women's National Alpine meet which was conducted at Stowe, VT. There Marion McKean (Wigglesworth) won the downhill and Grace Carter Lindley won the slalom. More disappointing to Gretchen was that she missed the '39 Harriman Cup which was held for the first time that year on Baldy.

For the '39 Harriman, which Gretchen missed due to her injury, Warm Springs run on Baldy had been cut thanks to the urging of Friedl Pfeifer who had taken over the Sun Valley Ski School. He solicited Kathleen Harriman, the founder's daughter, to help him persuade the boss that the future lay on that

Timberline Lodge finish line of the Golden Rose race on Mount Hood.

mountain. Otto Lang who had newly arrived from Mount Rainier to teach at Sun Valley also contributed to the selection of Baldy for development.

Although the Warm Springs trail had been cut, under the supervision of none other than Dick Durrance, in time for the race, the first lifts on Baldy were not put into use until the beginning of the following season. So the racers climbed the mountain both for practice and to race.

When Gretchen returned to racing in April 1939, near the end of the 1938–39 winter season, she finished with a respectable tenth in the Northwest Ski Championships at Mount Hood. She placed tenth even though she had not raced all season. That and her previous results qualified her for the 1940 Olympic team.

A month after these Northwest Championships, when the

Sun Valley, 1939, with Challenger Inn in background.

spring skiing of May, was at its height on Mount Rainier, Crown Prince Olav and Princess Martha of Norway came to Seattle on a state visit and brought along their own ski togs in anticipation of doing some skiing in the Cascades. Gretchen, with her Norwegian ancestry and having just been selected to the 1940 U.S. Olympic ski team, was asked to accompany the royal couple.

The Norwegian royal pair arrived with 90 trunks. They asked for skis to be sent to Paradise Inn on Mount Rainier for them. Once there, they proceeded to climb to Alta Vista for some American schussing. The prince had skied since he was two years old and was impressed with the skis sent up from Seattle. They had metal edges. He spent much of the time, however, talking about waxing which was the topic of the day for all connoisseurs of the sport. The sun was out and the photographers had a perfect opportunity.

A royal banquet was held at the Winthrop Hotel May 23, 1939, and Gretchen pasted the menu from it into her rapidly developing scrap book. She had never been to her mother's home in Norway, a visit she promised herself after the Olympics. Little did she know the Olympics for which she had been selected were soon to be canceled due to war. She did eventually get to Norway but not until the next Olympics which regrettably were not held until eight long years had passed.

On the bright side, before the snows of another ski season descended, six months after Averell Harriman's prescient announcement of their engagement, Don finally proposed. They were married in Seattle on October 14, 1939, just before the start of the 1939–40 ski season.

Bridesmaids for the Episcopal wedding were Claudia Von Fossen, Mary McDonald, Evelyn Hopkins, Mrs. Florence McLean with Virgina Haines as maid of honor.

Harriman had offered Don a job as sports director for the resort of Sun Valley. With the Olympics cancelled Don took it. After the wedding they left for the Union Pacific headquarters in Omaha, Nebraska and then embarked for what they hoped to be an extended honeymoon in Sun Valley. Don never raced internationally after that but Gretchen, with Don's urging, kept getting better and better.

The 1940 downhill of the Harriman Cup was once again held on Warm Springs Run on Baldy. It was a little wider this time because the trees the racers hit the previous year had been marked and were cut down that summer. But it still was not lift-served. However, on the River Run side of the mountain, inaugurated that winter, a three-stage lift system to the top of Baldy was put into service. So the racers only had to do a top-of-the-mountain traverse to get to the start gate of the Warm Springs race course. At least they did not have to climb the mountain any more—unless they wanted to do it for conditioning and course inspection.

(The first lifts on Baldy were constructed during the sum-

Gretchen on wedding day, October 14, 1939. PORTRAIT IN SCRAPBOOK

mer of 1939 on the River Run side of the mountain. In total they ascended 3,253 feet to the top of Baldy and were put into operation in December at the start of the '39–40 winter season.)

This was the year Durrance ran his famous hair-raising race and won his third Harriman race retiring the cup. To accomplish this he schussed the Steilhang shouting "Too fast, too fast." Pictures of him show him on one foot with the other going over a small pine tree.

At the banquet when Averell Harriman gave him the cup he also gave him the advice, "Never, never race like that again, Dick."[3]

Grace Lindley won the downhill that year with her skis on the wrong feet.

(Because of the way boots were mated to bindings in those days, she probably was unable to snowplow or stem as much as she might otherwise have.)

She decided to celebrate with a dip in the Lodge pool. As the downhill champion touched one toe in to test the water, a male guest lounging nearby asked, "Did you try skiing?" The distaff downhill champion replied nonchalantly, "Yes."[4]

Bill Janss, who was to buy the resort almost a quarter of a century later, came in 13th. Gretchen, now married and now racing for Sun Valley Ski Club, came in 5th in the downhill, llth in the slalom and 4th in the combined.

She ended the season by traveling to California where she won on April 21, 1940, the first Silver Belt Race at Sugar Bowl ski area in California. The appropriate trophy: a silver belt buckle. Friedl Pfeifer won the men's Silver Belt buckle.

(They were the first man and woman, in a long list of renowned racers to come after them through the years, to receive the prestigious California Silver Belt buckle. Gretchen's buckle—the first one awarded—is now in the Ketchum-Sun Valley Ski and Heritage Museum.)

The following season she won the combined 1941 Harriman Cup via an impressive first in the downhill.

Hollywood and big business executives such as Nestle's Chocolate heir, Tony Page, and Wilbur May of the department store fame, plus Nelson Rockefeller of New York, Robert Pabst of Milwaukee, Gary Cooper and Claudette Colbert and other Hollywood celebrities continued to flock to Sun Valley. At the mid-mountain Roundhouse the parties went on day and night—mostly at night. Champagne and caviar abounded. A few people even fell out of the night-time, down-mountain chair lift rides, which put an end to the on-mountain parties. The après skiers who stayed at the Lodge donned long dresses and ties to make grand entrances in the upstairs lodge dining room. Most elegant always was Norma Shearer, according to Gretchen, who first saw the movie star in a gold lamé long evening dress descending the marble steps of the Lodge dining room. [5]

Darryl F. Zanuck, head of Twentieth Century Fox, came to Sun Valley with his wife and three children about this time. Thanks to his desire to film another movie with Sonja Henie, Sun Valley and destination skiing received a big boost. His film, about a Norwegian refugee who is in hot pursuit of John Payne, a singer in Glenn Miller's band was titled "Sun Valley Serenade." [6]

Most of the pursuit takes place at a ski area while the band plays, "It Happened in Sun Valley." America fell in love with destination skiing and the sport increased in participants when it was released in 1941.

Behind the scenes there was a sub-plot to the movie going on. Otto Lang had been enticed to leave his job in Washington state to teach skiing at Sun Valley. He had never met Zanuck even though he worked filming the ski sequences for the previous Zanuck-Sonja Henie film, "Thin Ice."

Lang was enlisted to teach the movie mogul to ski and to help again with filming the ski footage for Zanuck's latest movie. There was one problem: Sonja still had not learned to ski so Gretchen Fraser was again enlisted for the action shots.

Hans Hauser, the original head of the ski school, doubled for movie star, John Payne. Gretchen had to volunteer her time on the film because she did not want to jeopardize her amateur ski racing status. A young male Sun Valley school-boy named Jack Simpson was enlisted as a supplemental stand-in when Gretchen had to leave for a race. All the interior shots were done in Hollywood.

(In 1992 Russian premier Mikhal Gorbachev, in the waning days of Soviet Communism, proclaimed "Sun Valley Serenade" one of his favorite movies, checking it out of the Russian state-run film library more often than any other American film.[7] Even over 55 years after its release, the movie classic is still shown daily in Sun Valley.)

Prior to the movie's filming, the storm clouds that continued each winter to gather over Baldy Mountain overshadowed a bigger tempest that was blowing on the European side of the Atlantic.

Norway had been slated to hold the 1940 World Ski Championships but they were cancelled as a result of German troops marching into Austria. The 1940 Winter Olympic Games originally scheduled for Sapporo, Japan were first moved to Finland when Japan invaded China. Then they too were canceled when Russia invaded Finland. On September 3, 1939, Britain and France declared war on Germany when that country invaded Poland, kicking off World War II.

Away from it all, on the other side of the world, America tried to hold an isolationist view of the Asian and European happenings. Ski races went on in the American mountains for a little while. In fact the team was already selected for the FIS Championships and the 1940 Winter Olympics. When these competitions were canceled the team members received certificates of their selection to the World Championships and United States Olympic squad. America was just starting to take winter ski vacations but the winds of impending war squelched that, too.

In 1941 the Frasers were living in Denver as Don was work-

SONJA HENIE and JOHN PAYNE in **"SUN VALLEY SERENADE"** with GLENN MILLER   A Twentieth Century Fox Picture

Fox publicity photo for "Sun Valley Serenade." The skiers are really Gretchen Fraser (left) and Hans Hauser.

ing in public relations for the Union Pacific field office. That March Gretchen entered the National Championships held in nearby Aspen and became U.S. National Champion via a 1st in downhill, 3rd in slalom and a 1st in the combined. The 22-year-old bride had made it all the way to the top spot in the nation.

She sent a Western Union telegram home to her parents—COLLECT. It read:

> Won National downhill with 11 sec. lead. Love, Gretchen

A Swiss mountaineer and avalanche authority , Andre Roch, had recommended to residents where to cut the first ski racing trail on Aspen Mountain.[8] It was on this run, called Roch Run, where Gretchen won the prestigious U.S. national title.

Gretchen also won, that same season, the 1941 Harriman Cup. It was presented to her by Otto Lang. In a peasant skirt and hair piled on top of her head, with an Edelweiss flower in it, she graciously accepted the cup from the ski instructor who had taught her to ski five years previously on Mount Rainier.

Then on December 8, 1941, just before a new ski season was to start, America entered the war. Now ski races were mostly regional in attendance because of gas rationing. One more Harriman Cup race was held and then curtailed for the duration.

Before they went overseas, some of the 10th Mountain Camp Hale ski troops came over to Alta, Utah for the 1942 Snow Cup giant slalom. Friedl Pfeifer, by then a corporal in the U.S. Army, won the 40-gate race. Gretchen Fraser led the women's competitors by a wide margin. More than half the race entrants for the men were in the military. Some of the former racers in the Camp Hale contingent entering the competition were Dev Jennings, Steve Knowlton and Tom Cremer.[9] All ski racing came to a halt at the end of that winter as America's war involvement increased.

Sun Valley's founder, Averell Harriman, had been conspicuously absent from the 1941 and '42 Harriman Cup races. Well known in the top echelon of government, he was across the Atlantic, deeply involved in negotiating American aid to Great Britain (The Lend Lease Plan). He so distinguished himself as a negotiator that President Roosevelt sent him, when America's war involvement escalated, to be the U.S. Wartime Ambassador to Russia. He served at this post from 1943 to 1946 taking his daughter, Kathleen, with him as hostess for his Moscow mission.

It was the start of a distinguished political and diplomatic career that was to take him further and further each year from his valley in the sun.

His Union Pacific resort and its racers all took on new wartime roles, too. Lives were changed but vivid memories endured of happy times with nothing more on the mind than to make the next two gates of a race course.

Wartime

T HE FRASERS HAD SETTLED in comfortably as Sun Valley locals when abruptly the radio in the Challenger Inn lobby blared out the news of America's entry into World War II. It was December 8, 1941: The Japanese had attacked Pearl Harbor the day before.

In a publicity boomerang, *Life* Magazine's pictures of charming Austrian ski instructors suddenly became the focus of an FBI hunt. Agents descended on remote Sun Valley for those Austrians. With their accents and outdoor good looks they had captured the hearts of many American women, but they could be spies. In fact the FBI was so sure of it that two days after Pearl Harbor, they carted off Hans Hauser (original ski school head), Sepp Froehlich and Friedl Pfeifer (then ski school director) as enemy aliens capable of sending shortwave messages to Germany—in between skiing down the mountain tops of the Sawtooths and chaperoning an assortment of female beauties up the ski lifts.

Friedl went first to Salt Lake City and then with Hans both were sent to Fort Lincoln, North Dakota. Sepp was interned in Salt Lake City and through his American heiress wife (Natalie Rogers of the Warburg banking family) demanded a hearing. When Friedl's wife, (Holt Smith, daughter of the president of the First Security Trust Company of Salt Lake City),

Gretchen with Don in his Navy uniform in Hollywood, Florida, during World War II. SNAPSHOT FROM SCRAPBOOK

heard of that she tried to do the same. Her father, Fred E. Smith, appeared providing officials with proper identification. Then President Jeffers of the Union Pacific Railroad and Pat Rogers, manager of Sun Valley wrote letters. To top it off, so did Averell Harriman. All vouched for his character and that secured Friedl's release.

Both Friedl and Sepp were released in mid-February (2½ months after their arrest and detainment). Friedl went back to

Sun Valley to head the ski school but alas the resort was on the brink of preparing to close for the duration. Patriotically, both Friedl and Sepp joined the American 10th Mountain Ski Troops.[1]

Hans went to enemy detention camp in Stringtown, Oklahoma where he was held in an old penitentary until the end of the war. His brother, Max, had previously left Sun Valley to return to German-occupied Austria where he had been a known Nazi sympathizer. Hans—whenever he was not skiing, or teaching . . . or socializing—might send him spy messages, so the FBI reasoned.

Through the winter of 1942 the movie stars continued to return to Sun Valley. The guest register read: Ann Southern, Norma Shearer, The Darryl Zanucks, Gary Cooper, Ray Milland and Claudette Colbert. Every afternoon after skiing guests and employees alike gathered in the Lodge's second floor reception room overlooking the ice rink and knitted sweaters and socks for the troops. Some people even knitted on the chairlifts.

A Home Guard Unit was formed and blackouts were initiated. America was sure if the Japanese invaded the country, the Rockies would be the U.S. stronghold and the enemy would be defeated on this front.

Don Fraser went to Pensacola, Florida, to teach gunnery as an ensign in the U.S.Navy. Gretchen went with him for a short time. As Sun Valley's sports director, Don knew about guns: he was an avid duck hunter and had taught guests the fine art of skeet shooting on the range of the resort's gun club. Representing Sun Valley he had competed in national trap shooting events. When Don went to the Pacific as a gunnery officer on the *Essex*, Gretchen went back to Sun Valley and then to Washington state.

The Idaho resort was still trying to operate. With gas rationing on, the sleigh that took guests to Trail Creek Cabin was fixed up to bring guests to Baldy for skiing, but it was no use. On December 20, 1943, just before the resort was to open for the season (with advanced reservations booked solid), its closure for the duration was announced.

In June, 1943, the Navy took it over as a recuperational hospital for the war-wounded. On July 1, 1943, it was commissioned by the Navy as: U.S. Naval Special Hospital, Sun Valley, Idaho. The hospital had a capacity of 1,800 enlisted men and 300 officers.[1]

Its purpose was the hospitalization, rehabilitation and recreation of servicemen. Furthermore its climate was said to help malaria victims. In total it administered to the mental and physical wounds of 6,578 Navy, Marine and Coast Guard patients during the three years of wartime service .

Deep in the woods beyond the hospital, Trail Creek Cabin was pressed into service as the Officers' Club.

Bing Crosby came to entertain the troops and stayed to do some fishing nearby. He was lodged beside the hospital in Harriman cottage, since the absentee founder of Sun Valley was overseas in wartime diplomatic service.

To bolster the morale of American citizens at home and at the front, Otto Lang started making highly patriotic films for RKO-Pathé in a series called "This is America." Gretchen was again asked to ski for Otto in one of these films and went to Alta, Utah. While there she saw the amputees returning from the war to Bushnell Hospital in Brigham, Utah. She promptly volunteered to teach them to ski in an effort to raise their spirits.

"I had no idea how to do it. I just figured there must be a way to help them enjoy life again and raise their confidence," said Gretchen to a newspaper reporter near Snow Basin in Utah.

It was the beginning of a life-long commitment to handicapped skiers—a cause she never wavered from, even after she won Olympic fame.

Many of the Sun Valley Ski Instructors and racers joined the military to serve in the 10th Mountain Ski Troops. Sigi Engl, who later became a long-time head of the ski school,

*Kathleen Harriman Mortimer and Gretchen Fraser in fur accessories from
Russia acquired during Averell Harriman's wartime ambassadorship there.*

found himself one day on the front lines which, at the first
light of dawn, looked familiar. He was at the foot of the hor-
rendous Abbetone downhill race course in the Appenines
where in 1935 he had won his last race before he left for
America. Ex-Dartmouth racer, Percy Rideout, and University

Mrs. Fraser Wins Title For Women

By Dick Movitz

Corporal Friedl Pfeifer, Camp Hale, Colo., led the standout field in the Jaycee Winter Sports club Snow Cup giant slalom at Alta Sunday as he threaded his way through the 40-gate slalom maze in a total time of 1:54, five seconds ahead of Jack Reddish, Alta Ski club, runner-up. Gretchen Fraser, former Sun Valley racer, led the women competitors by a large margin with an elapsed time of 1.55.1 over a shortened course.

Before nearly 2000 ski fans, the racers put on a show unequaled in previous intermountain ski competitions. With army skiers filling more than half the men's entries, the race had an added interest.

Following Pfeifer and Reddish in the men's race were Dev Jennings, Camp Hale and former Salt Lake skier, with 2:01.2; Steve Knowlton, Camp Hale and former Dartmouth carnival champion, with 2:03.2, and Tom Cremer, Camp Hale and former northwest class A racer, with 2:03.3. The first five in the men's class were awarded medals.

Behind Mrs. Fraser in the women's race were Shirley McDonald, Alta and formerly of Sun Valley, Idaho, with 1:55.1, and Mary Louise Stevenson, Salt Lake ski maiden, who was participating in her first ski race, with 2:11.3 The first three women finishers also received attractive medals.

The course started at the top of the second lift and finished at the floor of the basin. Martin Fopp, Alta ski professional, set the open, but treacherous, course.

Local skiers showed extremely well in the final standings. Pfeifer ran the race without a fall, displaying perfect control over the hard packed course. One of the top slalom racers in the world, he recently returned to Salt Lake on furlough after being off skis for nearly a year.

Reddish also ran a no-fall race to lead the local skiers. The young Granite high school junior showed, his heels to many of the top racers in the country. Fred Keller, local skier, finished sixth with 2:03 in an excellent run.

The Snow Cup trophy is donated by Herbert A. Snow, prominent Utah industrialist, and the slalom has been held for three seasons. Past winners were Barney McLean, national amateur champion, in 1940, and Dick Durrance, national champion in 1941. Mrs. Fraser has won the women's race on the two previous competitions.

Results:

Ladies:
1 Gretchen Fraser 1:33.1
2 Shirley MacDonald 1:55.1
3 Mary Lou Stephenson 2:11.3
4 Ann Brooks 2:20.0
5 Winifred Valens 2:41.3
6 Shirley Stranquist 2:42.1
7 Bette Tepper 3:11.1

Men:
1 Friedl Pfeifer 1:54.0
2 Jack Reddish 1:59.1
3 Devereaux Jennings 2:01.2
4 Stephen Knowlton 2:02.2
5 Tom Cremer 2:02.2
6 Fred Keller 2:03.3
7 Mack Maeser 2:03.0
8 Bill Bowes 2:06.2
9 Charley McLean 2:07.2
10 Ralph Ball 2:07.4
11 Bob Groesbeck 2:09.3
12 Don Goodman 2:09.4
13 Dick Movitz 2:09.4
14 Carl Stingl 2:12.3
15 Dick McCrudden 2:14.2
16 Merrill White 2:15.0
17 John Elvrum 2:15.1
18 Jerry Hiatt 2:15.4
19 Curt Chase 2:16.0
20 Dick Nebeker 2:16.2
21 Pat Kearnes 2:16.4
22 Abbott Phillips 2:17.3
23 Chuck Hibbard 2:19.0
24 Burdell Winter 2:19.3
25 Brigg Smith 2:19.3
26 Bill Bechdolt 2:19.4
27 Joseph Barrie 2:20.4
28 Ed Hornung 2:23.1
29 Henry Seidelhuber 2:23.2
30 Gage Chetwood 2:24.4
31 Ted Major 2:24.4
32 Tap Tapley 2:25.0
33 Leon Goodman 2:25.2
34 Bill Farrell 2:26.0
35 Bob Smith 2:27.0
36 Harold Goodro 2:30.3
37 Lewis Hauge 2:32.3
38 Mahon Wells 2:33.3
39 Erling Omland 2:37.0
40 Crosby Perry-Smith 2:40.3
41 Bernard Peters 2:44.2
42 Don Cutter 2:46.2
43 Dave Jones 2:54.0
44 Ralph Bromghan 2:57.2
45 George Goodman 2:59.1
46 Kay Smith 3:00.4
47 Gus Tepin 3:14.4
48 William Santee 3:17.4
49 Wendell Cram 3:19.4
50 Dick Westin 3:20.2
51 Dick Smith 3:29.2
52 Louis Hall 3:30.0
53 Robert Beck 3:48.1
54 Roger Edman 3:52.2
55 Arthur Earle 3:57.4

Snow Cup at Alta, 1942. Last race for the duration of the war.

of Washington racer, Bill Neidner, took part in the assault on German fortified positions on Riva Ridge, Italy. Steve Knowlton who had raced in the Harriman Cup probed German lines for weak spots.

The roster of 10th Mountain Ski Troops included Sun Valley residents: Ken Beck, Barney Becker, Barney Bell, Edmund Bennett, Nelson Bennett, Ralph Bromaghan, Gordon Butterfield, Dave Conger, Wendall Cram, Jack Colven, Bert Cross, Paul Duke, Joe Duncan, Fritz Ehrl, Sigi Engl, Leon Goodman, Don Goodman, Alex Gordon, Victor Gottschalk, Ted Chelton Leonard, John Litchfield, George Loudis, Donald Marburg, Tony Matt, Friedl Pfeifer, Freddy Pieren, Walter Prager, Phil Puchner, Dale Rank, Percy Rideout, Peter Riehl, Olaf Rodegard, Adolph Roubicek, James Saviers, Karl Stingl, Pepi Teichner, Frank Unamino and Lou Whitcher.

May 8, 1945, was VE day in Europe, followed (in August) by the surrender of the Japanese in the Pacific. The Navy moved out of Sun Valley and the resort reopened for business on December 21, 1946.

The Harriman Cup was resumed that season ('46–47) with dominance by European skiers. Edi Rominger, a member of the Swiss team was the men's winner and Georgette Thioliére from France captured the women's title.

The end of the war meant the resumption of the Olympics after an eight year suspension. While the game was the same, most of the players were unknowns. With only one season to prepare for the 1948 Olympics, there were no recent races as there are today to gauge one's international competition capabilities. But peace had come and a world full of hope prepared for the Vth Winter Olympics.

St. Moritz, Switzerland, site of the first Winter Olympics after World War II. SWISS NATIONAL TOURIST OFFICE

FOUR

Peace and The Olympics

WHEN THE WAR ENDED Don was offered a position as general manager of Sun Valley but the Frasers did not go back to living at the resort. Instead Don took over his uncle's gas and home heating oil distributorship in Vancouver, Washington. Gretchen did the bookkeeping and corresponded with the station managers. At first it was a struggle but the business under their direction kept the Frasers comfortably well off from then on. They vacationed in Sun Valley often.

In October 1947, a new run called Olympic, named in anticipation of the upcoming Winter Games, was commissioned at Sun Valley. It originated at the Roundhouse, proceeded northward intersecting with River Run at about midway. It was a popular free-ski run for the racers training for the 1948 U. S. Olympics because of its newness and convenient lift access. The Warm Springs side of Baldy, where The Olympic Downhill Tryout Races were held was still without lift service.

(It was not until the mid-1960s, when the eternal racer, Bill Janss, took over Sun Valley that the Warm Springs side of Baldy sprouted chair lifts.)

The racers rode the three River Run lifts and traversed over from the top of Christmas lift to get to the start gate. The Tryout Slalom was on Ruud Mountain, on the other side of the village from Baldy.

Sun Valley's River Run side (pictured here) was where the first lifts on Baldy were erected in the summer of 1939. Note blankets on chairs. Since the 1994–95 ski season this same site displays the confluence of four lifts 1) the upper terminal of the River Run detachable high-speed quad chair, 2) the loading station of the Exhibition triple lift, 3) the loading station the Lookout Express detachable high-speed quad chair to the top of the mountain, and 4) the loading station for the Sunnyside triple chair.

(To see Ruud Mountain in modern day drive out half way on mansion-studded Fairway Drive at Sun Valley. It is on the right hand side of the road. Some towers still remain of the old lift.)

For the 1948 Games six divisions of the U.S. Ski Association held regional tryout races. The U.S. team semi-final tryout races were held March 1 and 2 at Snow Basin, Utah. They were followed on March 16 by the final tryout races at Sun Valley. The Harriman Cup races, run that same week, were also taken into account by the Olympic Selection Committee.

Gretchen almost did not go to the tryouts. She had pulled herself away from the family business to go to Mount Hood for the Pacific Northwest Ski Association (PNSA) championships open tournament where she won straight firsts in downhill, slalom and combined. After being off skis for the war years (except for a few times making war effort movies and helping amputees to ski) she had somehow managed to retain her old form. At the urging of her husband she entered the Olympic tryout races held at Sun Valley. She was 27 years old and laughingly called herself a "retread."

The races at Sun Valley always drew a large crowd of participants including international competitors who came for the Harriman Cup. In the Harriman the glamourously feminine French racer, Georgette Thiolière, took the women's downhill, slalom and combined. *Life* Magazine featured her on its cover. With her always belted parka to cinch in her waist and her high turban she was movie-star glamourous and could out-ski most of the men.

As for the Americans, all the talk focused on a hot-shot 14-year old from Pico Peak, Vermont, named Andrea Mead. *Time* magazine put Andrea on the cover. But as the Olympic tryout races were held it was Gretchen who won the slalom on Ruud Mountain and the downhill on Warm Springs. The 27-year-old was followed by a spectacular second place by the 14-year-old Andrea.

"They had to take me (on the team)," joked the Retread. "After all I had won."[1]

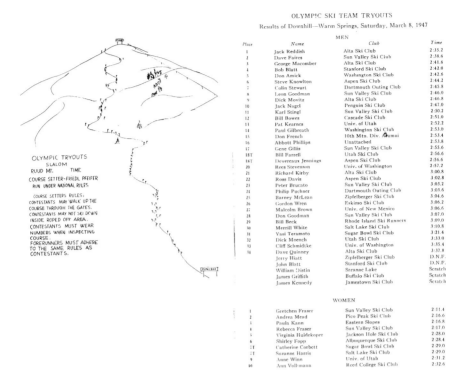

OLYMPIC SKI TEAM TRYOUTS
Results of Downhill—Warm Springs, Saturday, March 8, 1947

MEN

Place	Name	Club	Time
1	Jack Reddish	Alta Ski Club	2:35.2
2	Dave Faires	Sun Valley Ski Club	2:38.6
3	George Macomber	Alta Ski Club	2:41.6
4	Bob Blatt	Stanford Ski Club	2:42.0
5	Don Amick	Washington Ski Club	2:42.6
6	Steve Knowlton	Aspen Ski Club	2:44.2
7	Colin Stewart	Dartmouth Outing Club	2:45.8
8	Leon Goodman	Sun Valley Ski Club	2:46.0
9	Dick Movitz	Alta Ski Club	2:46.8
10	Jack Nagel	Penguin Ski Club	2:47.0
11	Karl Stingl	Sun Valley Ski Club	2:50.2
12	Bill Bowes	Cascade Ski Club	2:51.0
13	Pat Kearns	Univ. of Utah	2:52.2
14	Paul Gilbreath	Washington Ski Club	2:53.0
15	Don French	10th Mtn. Div. Alumni	2:53.4
16	Abbott Phillips	Unattached	2:53.8
17	Gene Gillis	Sun Valley Ski Club	2:55.6
18T	Bill Farrell	Utah Ski Club	2:56.6
18T	Devereaux Jennings	Aspen Ski Club	2:56.6
20	Rees Stevenson	Univ. of Washington	2:57.2
21	Richard Kirby	Alta Ski Club	3:00.8
22	Ross Davis	Aspen Ski Club	3:02.8
23	Peter Brucato	Sun Valley Ski Club	3:03.2
24	Philip Puchner	Dartmouth Outing Club	3:03.6
25	Barney McLean	Zipfelberger Ski Club	3:04.6
26	Gordon Wren	Eskimo Ski Club	3:06.2
27	Malcolm Brown	Univ. of New Mexico	3:06.6
28	Don Goodman	Sun Valley Ski Club	3:07.0
29	Bill Beck	Rhode Island Ski Runners	3:09.0
30	Merrill White	Salt Lake Ski Club	3:10.8
31	Vasi Teramoto	Sugar Bowl Ski Club	3:21.4
32	Dick Moench	Utah Ski Club	3:33.0
33	Cliff Schmidtke	Univ. of Washington	3:35.4
34	Dave Quinney	Alta Ski Club	3:37.8
	Jerry Hiatt	Zipfelberger Ski Club	D.N.F.
	John Blatt	Stanford Ski Club	D.N.F.
	William Distin	Saranac Lake	Scratch
	James Griffith	Buffalo Ski Club	Scratch
	James Kennedy	Jamestown Ski Club	Scratch

WOMEN

1	Gretchen Fraser	Sun Valley Ski Club	2:11.4
2	Andrea Mead	Pico Peak Ski Club	2:16.6
3	Paula Kann	Eastern Slopes	2:16.8
4	Rebecca Fraser	Sun Valley Ski Club	2:17.0
5	Virginia Huldekoper	Jackson Hole Ski Club	2:28.0
6	Shirley Fopp	Albuquerque Ski Club	2:28.4
7T	Catherine Corbett	Sugar Bowl Ski Club	2:29.0
7T	Suzanne Harris	Salt Lake Ski Club	2:29.0
9	Anne Winn	Univ. of Utah	2:31.2
10	Ann Vollmann	Reed College Ski Club	2:32.6

OLYMPIC TRYOUTS
SLALOM
RUUD MT.   TIME
COURSE SETTER—FRIEDL PFEIFER
RUN UNDER NATIONAL RULES

COURSE SETTERS RULES:
CONTESTANTS MAY WALK UP THE
COURSE THROUGH THE GATES.
CONTESTANTS MAY NOT SKI DOWN
INSIDE ROPED OFF AREA.
CONTESTANTS MUST WEAR
NUMBERS WHEN INSPECTING
COURSE.
FORERUNNERS MUST ADHERE
TO THE SAME RULES AS
CONTESTANTS.

The Olympic Tryouts slalom race course map and Olympic Tryouts downhill race results. AMERICAN SKI ANNUAL, 1948

Friedl Pfeifer, her co-winner in the Sugar Bowl Sliver Belt (California) and Alta Snow Cup (Utah) races before the war, had set the slalom for the Olympic team tryout course. The slalom expert reasoned that the Swiss would play it safe and set a conventional course at the Olympics in St. Moritz —one much tighter than those used in the American West. So that is how he set it. (See his sketch which was supplied to the racers) The Ruud Mountain course was declared a "wholly adequate test but somewhat conventional."[2] (The writer thought it required sharper turns between gates than those set for usual Western races)

(The mountain was named after veteran skier Birger Ruud of Norway, who in 1932 won an Olympic gold medal in jumping and in 1936 won another Olympic gold in jumping. That same year he also won the downhill portion of the combined event.

Despite the unusualness of winning both a jumping and a downhill event in the Olympic Games of '36, he took home only one medal—for jumping—because in this first-ever Olympics to have alpine competitions, downhill was linked to slalom results for a medal in the combined event.)

The 1947 Olympic tryout downhill on Baldy's Warm Springs, was a racer-familiar drop of 3,100 feet over a distance of 2-5/8 miles. The men started at the top and the women at the Steilhang, some 400 vertical feet lower and 3,000 feet shorter.

(Few people ski the Steilhang today except The Masters class. Advanced classes go there when new snow conditions are right. It is never groomed. To ski the Steilhang in modern times, start down International Run. When it begins to turn toward Warm Springs, keep going straight through the trees. It turns and enters Warm Springs lower on the mountain.)

In early Harriman days, snow grooming on the mountain was the human kind rather than the modern machinery kind. After a big snow storm the entire ski school would gather at the top of Baldy and ski perfect S-turns all the way down, cautiously looking over their shoulders in fear of an oncoming avalanche or a fellow instructor. For the race courses side stepping was employed because they were narrower. Such was the state-of-the-art for snow grooming and avalanche control in the 1940s.

The women selected to the team were: Dodie Post (Captain), Gretchen Fraser, Paula Kann, Brynhild Grasmoen, Andrea Mead, Ruth-Marie Stewart, Rebecca Cremer and Ann Winn. Alice Kiaer was appointed their manager. Suzanne Harris was also selected as an alternate but stayed home.

Walter Prager, twice winner of the Arlberg-Kandahar races before becoming ski coach of the Dartmouth ski team and Alf

Engen, several times U.S. national ski champion, were appointed men's coaches, but there was no coach designated for the women. They were told to get physically fit on their own over the summer and admonished not to wear high heels, so as to stretch the Achilles tendons.

For the Vth Winter Games to be held in Switzerland, the U.S. Olympic Committee gave permission for the teams to go to Europe by either plane or boat for approximately a six week period preceding the Games. Both the men and women team members met in New York three days before departure and sailed on December 8. The plan was to go to Davos and take short trips to enter competitions and then go to St. Moritz on January 13 to practice on the Olympic courses before they were closed prior to the Games. A total budget of approximately $47,656 was to cover the advance training period and expenses.[3]

Gretchen left Seattle by train along with men's team members Dave Faires and Don Amick. As a send off there was a pre-Olympic fund-raising dance held in Seattle's Palladium ballroom under the direction of Gus Eriksen with Mel Borgerson assisting.

As the western-most Olympians traveled across country other team members got on the same train. Olympic excitement ran high as the train chugged across America's heartland.

On arriving at the other end of the country, Gretchen planned on spending a few days with her friend, newly married Kathleen Harriman Mortimer. "Kathy" was in charge of uniforms for the team and had collected an impressive wardrobe designed by Fred Picard of Picard's of Sun Valley. Jantzen did the grey worsted gabardine ski suits and there were poplin parkas with fur trim plus hand-knit sweaters by Marjorie Benedickter. Most impressive were wool alpaca coats, long black après ski skirts and chic pure silk scarfs decorated with delightfully drawn skiers which Max Barsis—Sun Valley's official watercolorist and cartoonist-in-residence—had dreamed

Gretchen about time of the Olympic Tryouts, 1947.

At Aspen, Colorado, 1947 (from left) Jerry Hiatt, Barney McClean, Friedl Pfeifer, French racer Georgette Thiolière and (boarding chair) Alleen Robison. ASPEN HISTORICAL SOCIETY

up. As the ski suits did not come with belts Gretchen added her own belt with the buckle she had won in the initial California Silver Belt race at Sugar Bowl in 1940.

Each woman was issued several pair of skis. The brands were Northland, Gregg, and Groswold. Lastly each was given a "bustle basket." The latter is known as a "fanny pack" today.

Gretchen and Kathleen had a private lunch between uniform and boot fittings. Then they went to Kathleen's apartment where Gretchen met for the first time Kathy's husband, Stanley Mortimer.

Gretchen had started an Olympic diary. The December 5, 1948, entry reads:

> *Late into New York. Kathy came to meet me then back to Olympic committee rooms. Got to Kathy's apartment at 5. Met Stan. He is so nice.*

Four of the racers named to the American 1948 team pose at Sun Valley after the tryout race. From left: Gretchen Fraser, Andrea Mead, Paula Kann, Brynhild Grasmoen. SUN VALLEY CO.

Meanwhile over in Europe the world racers had already assembled. At the first snow of the season the French team left for Alsace assembling near Strasbourg for intensive conditioning. Twenty-seven Italian ski team members were getting acclimated near the Matterhorn. The Austrian team with 20 pair of Attenhofer skis converged in early November on the Zugspitze near Garmisch. (The Austrian ski factories were still recovering from the effects of war-production materiels so the Austrians were using Swiss Attenhofer skis. Furthermore, their cunning strategy was to train on the border-hugging German Zugspitze because of its high altitude (2,966 meters), which has a similar altitude as the 3,026 meter Piz Nair of St. Moritz where the downhill was to be staged. It was not until 1949 when the West German Federal Republic was formed and the Marshall Plan was inaugurated, to rebuild Europe, that the Austrians started rebuiling their ski factories. Ironically, none other than W. Averell Harriman was apppointed administrator of The Marshall Plan).

The Swiss already had their team in St. Moritz training since the beginning of November. German ski racers were nowhere to be seen. Germany, as in the aftermath of World War I, had been disbarred from the 1948 Olympics.

On the other side of the Atlantic, in stark contrast, the American Alpine and Nordic ski teams of 17 men and eight women sailed December 8 on the *S. S. America.*

(It was like they were on a slow boat to Europe even though the *S.S. America* was one of the fastest ocean liners of its day. When I added the total travel days from the time Gretchen left Seattle to when she hit the Swiss mountains, it was 18 days. She boarded a train in Seattle to ride for five days and nights to New York. She spent three days in New York for uniform and boot fittings, then sailed across the Atlantic for 10 more days, followed by an overnight train to Paris and then spent two days on a narrow gauge railroad getting to the mountains. TOTAL: 18 travel days. In modern times the same trip takes less than 18 hours.) Gretchen chronicled it all in her diary. Some of the entries follow:

> *December 8 on S.S. America:*
> *Cabin class M58. Two port holes. By dinner time two members ill.*

> *December 12 on S. S. America:*
> *Sick in bed.*

> *December 15 on train Cherbourg to Paris:*
> *We received our bread ration cards.*

December 16 after overnight in Paris:
Got up at 5. Breakfast at 5:30. Narrow gauge
railroad to Davos.

December 18 (Davos, Flüela Hotel)
No one skied at all well. Too much sea legs. Like my
Groswolds. Pictures. Dinner. Skied with Prince of
Liechtenstein who is a good skier. Tea at Palace.
Tonight to concert.

December 19:
Dodie broke leg. Sad day.

December 24:
Downhill practice at Pontresina in morning.
Most teams scratched. Andy 1st; Ruth and I with
terrific spill at end.

December 25:
Parties. Tables with Swiss and American flags.
Waxing irons given all for Christmas. Sleigh home.
Eighteen in two sleighs.

The team was away from home for Christmas but members exchanged gifts limited to six francs each. Men's team member, Steve Knowlton of Colorado, presided as Santa Claus.

"He was a good and very humorous Santa Claus," wrote Gretchen in a letter to her parents at home, a half a world away, in Tacoma.

(This is the same Colorado Ski Country Steve Knowlton who reigned for so many post-war years as the exuberant master of ceremonies in the rollicking night club he owned called the Golden Horn in Aspen. Few people know how he got his center-stage start playing Santa when he was on the '48 Olympic Ski Team.)

The $47,656 budget did not include a coach for the women, so the men's downhill team was asked to coach them—a different man each day for eight days. With the various coaches everyone was getting mixed-up. Eight different techniques were taught by each of eight men.

The women's manager, Alice Kiaer, recognizing the situation, prevailed on the generosity of Don Momand, an American living in St. Moritz, to come up with funds to finance a coach for the orphan women's team. Thus, a Swiss slalom specialist, Walter Haensli, was hired. From then on things were easier because Walter spent evenings teaching waxing techniques. Also the team did not have to wander all over the mountain looking for the race courses. As an additional plus, the Swiss coach came from a family of five sisters so he related to the eight women team members easily.

Only one of the woman team members, Paula Kann (originally from Switzerland), had been to Europe before. So Walter entered the women in pre-Olympic races in Davos, Pontresina, Grindelwald and Klosters. Gretchen won the slalom at Klosters. The trophy was a cow bell given by the burgomaster. In presenting it he said to Gretchen, "I hope it brings you good luck."

(When Gretchen died in 1994 that cow bell was still hanging on the back of the front door of the Fraser's final home at Elkhorn in Sun Valley.)

Twenty-eight nations and 932 athletes gathered at St. Moritz in the Canton of the Grissons for the first postwar Winter Olympic Games. In total, St. Moritz Dorf (old) and St. Moritz Bad (new) had accommodations for 5,000 guests. Officials, athletes and press took 2,000 spaces leaving 3,000 spectator spaces, which were at a premium. A single room was $10/day. Gas was $0.65/gal.

(That same year gasoline was .18/gal in the U.S. and a room at Ski Tip Ranch at Arapahoe, Colorado, cost $3.50/day which included breakfast and dinner.)

There was only one night club then, the Chesa Veglia, located in a Romansch mountain home. Formal attire was required at the Suvretta, Kuhn, Carlton and Palace hotels. Horse drawn sleighs supplemented by 58 buses were the primary means to get around, day and night. Even Switzerland, which had remained neutral throughout the war, had not recovered its effects on automobile production.

In a letter to her parents dated January 16 Gretchen wrote:

My neglect in writing is really because we have been so busy. Today up at 7:30, breakfast at 8, waxed skis and out at nine. It snowed 8 inches in the night and dawned bright and clear. We went to the slalom slope and practiced until noon . . . worked in the wax room until 9:30 pm.

The letter was continued two days later, January 18:

Yesterday we had tea with Charles de Chateau of Belgium. He took us all home in his car, and cars are a rarity here. I noticed people looking at the car so finally asked him what it was. It was a 1948 Rolls Royce. He let me drive it but I like our Pontiac better . . . Our new coach has turned out to be a gem. In two days all skiing 100% better. . . .

The Swiss organizers were ready; they had already staged a winter Olympics in 1928. For the first time an electric-eye timing system was deployed. Now race results could be timed down to a hundredth of a second.

The courses for the events of the alpine combined were set at various points along the flank of the great open-slope of the east-facing mountain that rises from the village and hotel-bordered lake of St. Moritz. The women's downhill started at Piz Nair coming down the south face of the Corviglia funicular line, somewhat on the diagonal over the rolling open slopes where most of the recreational skiing at St. Moritz was done.

It finished on a little plateau, Salastrains. The slaloms were set above the Suvretta Hotel north of the Suvretta.

Competitors were pleased that the Olympic Committee inaugurated the plan of having two separate slaloms; one combined with the downhill for a combined medal and one, a special slalom, on the next day for another medal. Those were the only two medal-producing alpine events. The system would allow for specialization and at the same time retain the higher place of honor for the skier who could excel in both types of race. It also meant that the top finishers in downhill could enter a slalom in which they need not hold back to protect combined leads.

A young Swiss FIS official, Marc Hodler, set the slalom courses with the help of experts from the coaching staffs of the principal teams. The results were courses which were a compromise between the tight slaloms which the Swiss liked and the open ones such as Americans used.

Another innovation was that the men's and women's slalom events were run at the same time on separate but parallel courses.

Furthermore, the Europeans had developed a chemical for hardening the snow on race courses to prevent rutting. Supplies of this were on hand but they were not used. The diligent Swiss had shoveled away excess snow that fell in January and then turned a fire hose on the slope and foot tramped it. When new snow fell on this ice base they tramped it again into a surface nearly as hard as a diamond.

Caution prevailed among the competitors as the injury list mounted.

Canada's Rhoda Wurtele chipped her ankle and couldn't race. Her twin sister Rhona gamely entered the downhill where she fell but fought to the finish on what proved to be a broken leg. American team captain, Dodie Post was sidelined with injuries.

The stone-hard surface of the slalom course managed to upset some great reputations. French racer, Georgette Thiolière, who dazzled in America the prior season, failed to place. Another favored to win, Celina Seghi — Italy's "little squirrel"— hooked a ski in the 18th gate and stopped trying. The Austrians seemed unbeatable. But then there was a lone American, Gretchen Fraser.

She was alone in more ways than one. Her husband had not been able to leave the family business to accompany her to the games. Other obstacles prevailed: she was the oldest member of the team. She was, moreover, on a team which was not expected to do anything. Reporters never came over to their hotel for interviews. When someone with American press credentials met them he said, "Oh if someone breaks a leg, let us know and we'll send that (story) home ." Gretchen started to get mad, as if that was the only newsworthy event expected of the team.

George Trevar, North American Newspaper Alliance (NANA), wrote:

"Though American girl skiers are easier on the eyes than most of the foreign competitors (Miss Grasmoen is pretty enough to rate a Hollywood starlet role) the blunt truth is that our feminine slalom and downhill entrants haven't much of a chance at St. Moritz against the daredevil Wurtele twins of Canada and the accomplished Mlle. Georgette Thiolière of France."

The big pre-Olympic story was "Sabotage!"

During the night preceding the 2-man bobsled competition, some unknown person or persons gained admittance to the garage where USA bobsleds were housed and inflicted considerable damage to some of the sleds. On the 2-man sled, the steering wheel nut was loosened to the point where it would be likely to come off during the competition and, furthermore, the hood of the sled was bashed in by some heavy object. The steering wheels of other sleds had been tampered with, too. The culprits were never found.[4] The American ski team locked its ski wax room after that.

The alpine combined races were run first. For the down-hill part Hedy Schlumegger of Wengen, Switzerland won despite a momentarily sit-down fall. Austrians Trude Beiser and Rese Hammerer finished second and third respectively. Celina Seghi of Italy skied uncharacteristically cautiously and finished fourth.

Gretchen's downhill time was 13th just behind team mate Brynhild Grasmoen with a good 12th. It seemed to confirm that the U.S. team was not to be in the winners circle. Gretchen was depicted simply as a serious-minded girl from Mount Rainier and Sun Valley who had won the American championship and had always been "steady" in the race course.

She sent a dejected telegram to Don in Vancouver, Washington. It read:

Thirteenth in downhill, 8 seconds after winner. Wax slow.
Your Gretchen.

The press seemed to think she was not a force to be considered—an ascertainment which made her even madder. But she remained calm once she had the downhill completed and in two days would set the record straight.

The slalom part of the combined was a 37-gate course with a 575 foot drop. It was a day for the Austrians and for a lone American.

Despite her downhill setback Gretchen remained calm. "She looked so dead-pan cool, and so completely at ease that rivals all developed jitters, lost their heads and messed up runs," wrote James Laughlin filing a story for *Town and Country* magazine.

Erika "Riki" Mahringer had two perfect runs for a brilliant combined slalom first but the downhill proved her nemesis. Trude Beiser (with a second in the downhill) skied cautiously to a combined Olympic gold medal. Her rival in the slalom was Gretchen Fraser who tied with her on the first of the two-run slalom competition part for the combined. She did not know the American who was not a force in her book.

Gretchen and her Groswold skis get a 2nd in the combined at the 1948 Winter Olympics.

Yet when the downhill and two-run slalom results were tallied the unknown American, who was right on her tail in the first slalom run and had the faster time on the second slalom run, won a silver in the combined.

Who was Gretchen? Americans simply were not supposed to win medals in alpine skiing. She had been so little reckoned with she had to be pointed out time and again to the Olympic press. Was the silver medal a quirk of fate?

To those who knew Gretchen—like Otto Lang who taught her to ski on Mount Rainier and Friedl Pfeifer who raced and collected trophies with her in the pre-war races—she was grace under pressure.

Now she telephoned Don with the news then wrote a simple entry in her diary.

> *February 4:*
> *I came in second in the (combined) slalom, a great surprise to me and everyone else. Also got a (silver) 2nd in the combined. Lots of pictures. Did broadcasts and many interviews.*[5]

The special slalom was the next day. New bib numbers were drawn and Gretchen drew bib number one. It was not an enviable position—first racer on the course. There were so few forerunners she could not tell the state of the surface of the course. Moreover, there were no high tech communications gadgets from the bottom to relay coaches' messages up to her as she stood at the top of the course at Suvretta. Yet, she skied the first run deftly making no mistakes, to make sure she would be around for run number two.

The French women with lifted *ruades* chattered through the turns while Gretchen employed the smooth Arlberg that went right back to Lang and Pfeifer. Her judgement was perfect: a compromise between dash and care; between "letting go" and a steady, steady descent. The result of run number one for Gretchen was 59.7 sec.

Could the others beat it?

She waited for Mahringer who ran right after her. Time: 59.8. Then came Thiolière and Antoinette Meyer at 60.7 sec

Austria's Riki Mahringer (left) and Gretchen after their second run
of the Special Slalom. Since they were the first two racers down the
course, neither knew, when the photo was taken, that they had raced
to a bronze medal and a gold medal, respectively.
OVOMALTINE (AUSTRIA) RIKI MAHRINGER COLLECTION

The world waits at the finish line (left to right): May Nilsson of Sweden (with a 2nd run time the same as Gretchen's); Italy's "Little Squirrel," Celina Seghi (who was favored to win based on her pre-Games record); Austria's Erica Mahringer (with a 2nd-run time of 58.2 to add to a 1st-run time of 59.8); and Gretchen Fraser, USA, with a 2nd-run time of 57.5, besting her own 1st-run time of 59.7. There were thirty racers yet to come down the course, including Antoinette Meyer, who had the fastest time (57.0) of the day.
RIKI SPIESS-MAHRINGER COLLECTION

and within striking distance. Gretchen knew she was ahead on the first run but one little skid or one check in a crucial spot on the second run could wipe out her scant lead. As the racers trudged up to the top again she had the added pressure of knowing all eyes were on her.

"The course is worse than yesterday," she took the time to answer unruffled a reporter's question as she plodded back up for the second run.

The rules back then dictated that Gretchen again start first on the second run. She stepped into the gate, crouched and waited for the start. She waited . . . and waited. The new-fangled timing system had gone down. The malfunction was in the telephone connection that was part of the total unit.

Officials and coaches milled about, agitated. Gretchen waited in the gate staying focused. The delay ran into one minute, then two . . . then five. The racer with a silver medal from the day before stayed focused.

After ten minutes, the starter allowed her out of the gate to stretch her leg muscles.

Sidelined with injuries, U.S. team member, Dave Faires (who knew Gretchen from the Sun Valley races), found her and told her to take it easy. He knew she had a .1 second lead but four others were within 1.1 seconds of her first run. Any of their totals could count.

Then she was rushed back to the start gate. Finally after 17 minutes the timer was fixed but the forerunner was mysteriously missing so Gretchen had to plunge off cold without benefit of seeing someone else take the gates before her. The run changed her life forevermore.

Otto Lang watched the race and remembered Gretchen years later as coming down with "perfect composure" in one of those great enactments of "grace under pressure" to which all athletes aspire.

She sped through the finish banner, pigtails flying in the Alpine air. Gretchen had bested her own first run with a 57.5. But she had to wait some more, however, while 45 other competitors after her, skied the same course.

Mahringer of Austria was smooth again but seven-tenths slower at 58.2 sec.

Scratch her off.

The French Georgette slugged at every gate fighting for lost supremacy but even though she did not trip up, she was out of the medals.

Scratch her off.

May Nilsson of Sweden came in with the same time as Gretchen but her first run wiped her out of the running.

Scratch her off.

Those who could visually follow the second hand of the

Omega timing clock, held their breath as Lucienne Couttet was clocked, on the upper part of the course, with a speed faster than Gretchen. She was "going all out" when near the end on the last steep gate she straddled a flag and had to fight for 10 seconds to get untangled.

Scratch her off; breathe again.

Antoinette Meyer uncorked a whopper with the fastest time (57.0) of the day . She had gained a half second on Gretchen but combined with her first run could not beat Gretchen's two-run total. Her feat was almost as "impossible" as Gretchen's.

An American had won gold in the special slalom of the Vth Winter Olympics. When the medals were handed out it was Gretchen Fraser, gold; Antionette Meyer,silver; and Erica Mahringer, bronze.

All of gold's glitter was on Gretchen but the rest of the American women had dazzled on the slopes too. America's Mead, Grasmoen and Kann all put together remarkable runs for 8th, 10th and 11th respectably in the special slalom. History should not overlook their feats.

No one had thought to give protocol training to team members in talking to the press, as is done now, but Gretchen came by it naturally.

Still panting she told one AP reporter "I trained at Sun Valley." The next day, around the world Sun Valley had more publicity than dynamo Steve Hannegan could have ever dreamed up. The resort was on the ski destination maps forevermore. As far as Hannegan & Associates were concerned she was to be referred to as Gretchen Fraser of Sun Valley, Idaho regardless of the fact that she lived and continued to live in Vancouver, Washington. She raced for the Sun Valley Ski Club and, after all, had trained in Sun Valley before the war when she lived there.

When newspaper photographers flocked to take her victory pictures, Gretchen discarded her chewed up Groswold skis for new ones in deference to her friend Thor

Erica "Riki" Spiess-Mahringer in the fur-trimmed
parka Gretchen gave her in St. Moritz in 1948.
"Gretchen was a wunderbar Lady," wrote the
Austrian (in her seventies and living in Mayrhofen)
enclosing this well-carried photo for this book. RIKI
SPIESS-MAHRINGER COLLECTION

Groswold. The pigtails—she could not do anything about
them.

She later explained to her Norwegian relatives who wanted
to know about those "pigs' tails" thinking she carried some
sort of good luck charm from a swine. They had never heard
the word, pigtails. To them it had a vulgar translation. Gretchen
explained that they were braids and she wore her hair that way
because the traveling and the training did not allow extra time
to go to beauty parlors to have her hair done.

That day around the world the word spread thusly:

*Gretchen holding her two Olympic medals receives congratulations
from Hungarian IOC member, Dr. Ferano Mezo, February 5, 1948.*

"In a surprise upset a pigtailed western America housewife
named Gretchen Fraser, 28, who trained at Sun Valley, Idaho racked
up a gold in the special slalom of the Vth Winter Olympics..." *or*
"A pretty western housewife her pigtails flying accomplished something no American ever had done before—win
an Olympic medal for skiing . . ."

Gretchen at the finish line talked to reporters as if she had
been trained for it all her life. Such quotes as these flashed
around the world.

"I wasn't thinking of winning any medal. I just wanted to
do my best," she said with the red ribbons still on her pigtails.

Asked how she felt, she replied, "You don't have to worry
after you get underway . . ." or "I had no idea I could do it.
My husband will be very happy."

The new timing clock employed by the Swiss. REGIONAL HISTORY DEPT., COMMUNITY LIBRARY, KETCHUM, IDAHO, UNION PACIFIC COLLECTION

Her blonde pigtails and gracious manner won international attention.

When another AP reporter wrote: "She is blonde, pretty, proficient, and strangely inclined to humbleness . . ." everyone fell a little in love with the "unknown" American.

Getting ready. One silver and before the gold.

Immediately after the race at Suvretta there was a traffic jam of buses and sleighs. She had no idea how to get back to St. Moritz (about one mile away) when through the crowd Gretchen saw a decorated milk wagon drawn by a familiar pony. As it came closer Gretchen was amazed. It was the same pony she had been feeding sugar cubes to on her way to practice each morning as she left her hotel prior to the win. Enam-

Running: On course

ored with horses from childhood, she had been saving the breakfast sugar cubes (which were still rationed) each day to feed the pony in a nearby field. Now a farmer and his milk wagon pulled by the same pony had come to take America's new golden girl on her triumphant ride back to the Olympic village.[6]

"It was the closest I came to crying after I won." revealed Gretchen.[7]

Among the fondest memories of the Olympics were the sincere congratulations received from the racers whom she had beaten. Many of the foreign teams—some even our war-time enemy only a few years previously— gave her gifts. As she had four pairs of skis, she gave the Austrian contestants some of her equipment from America, thereby jump-starting her own version of the Marshall Plan. To Riki Mahringer she gave her team-issue fur trim parka which the Austrian racer declared, in a letter written almost 50 years later, that it always meant very much to her to have received it.

(From the war-ravished Austrian Olympic Committee, for her bronze medal showing, Riki received: 5kg *paket zucker.* Translation: an 11 lb bag of sugar. The sugar was supplied by the United Nations food-relief organization.)

The Swedish team skipped tea to bring Gretchen an orchid. Italy's Celina Seghi came up to her and said, "With your style you deserve to win."

"The generous way in which the other teams received my victory was touching and something I will never forget. I believe ...the sportsmanship in the Olympics is wonderful and especially among skiers," recalled Gretchen years later.[8]

Otto Lang writing for the *Seattle P-I* said, "Her room resembles nothing less than a florist's showroom. It is simply a mass of flowers. How proud Don must be . . ."

U. S. General One of Gretchen's Fans

Mrs. Gretchen Fraser of Vancouver, Wash., is congratulated by Maj. Gen. F. W. Milburn of Missoula, Mont., commander of the First U. S. infantry division in Bavaria, after she won high point honors for the American skiers in the Winter Olympics with a first in the special slalom and second in the Alpine combined downhill and slalom. (Associated Press Photo)

Gretchen and the General. ASSOCIATED PRESS PHOTO ARCHIVES

The 1948 U.S. Ladies Ski Team, left to right: Coach Walter Haensli, Gretchen Fraser, Paula Kann, Capt. Dodie Post, Manager Mrs. Alice Kiaer, Brynhild Grasmoen, Andrea Mead, Ruth Marie Stewart, Rebecca Cremer and Anne Winn. FOTO BY BUCHER

Meanwhile back in Vancouver, Washington it was impossible for anyone at Perkins Oil Co. (later changed to Don Fraser Co.) to get any work done. The telephone kept ringing with congratulations from people near and far. Finally Gretchen's call got through. As the media swarmed around the girl from the golden West, reporters also descended on Don Fraser in Vancouver, Washington. His big-smile photo reading the newspaper headlines of Washington newspapers was flashed across the country with the title: "Happiest Man in America."

Gretchen had called after she had won the silver. The phone call after the gold was much longer. "I most certainly am the happiest man in America," said Don . "It is a swell birthday present," he reiterated. (The win was five days before their shared birthdays of February 11).

Her parents in Tacoma were besieged too. They were quoted in newspapers attributing their daughter's success to co-ordination of mind and muscle.

Winning

The bells at the Sun Valley Opera House were ringing too. In St. Moritz there were parties by visiting American movie stars (Paulette Goddard, Burgess Meredith) and European royalty (the prince of Liechtenstein). Gretchen was asked to make a film in Switzerland with Edi Reinalter, the winner of the men's special slalom, who had received a much photographed congratulatory kiss from her. She never did make that movie.

Climbing Rainier slopes with Norwegian royalty in 1939
*left to right, Gretchen, Crown Prince Olav, and
Ole Berner of Oslo*

*When Gretchen was invited to a royal audience by the Crown Prince of
Norway following her gold medal Olympic win, Prince Olav showed
her this photo taken when he had skied with her on Mt. Rainier.*

American occupation forces in Bavaria had lined the courses
cheering for their country's racers. Gretchen, after her silver medal,
was quick to graciously say to Maj. Gen. Frank Milburn, of
Missoula, Montana—the commander of the First U.S. Infantry
division in Bavaria—"Your boys are our best boosters." After
that she was a bit of everyone's hometown gal for American overseas troops and the cheers for the U.S. team grew even louder.

Years later Gretchen recalled that the only press person to
troop up to the start gate before her winning run was Red
Barber. After the win, the media crowded in around her. Coach

Haensli being Swiss translated the newspaper accounts from the various European papers the next day. The owner of the Palace Hotel had a multi-lingual secretary and she was sent to help with the translations, too. Later an American business man helped answer the letters and cables.

Gretchen saved the headlines in her scrap book. They referred to her as: Pigtailed Housewife , Galloping Gretchen , Fetchen Gretch, and (for some unknown reason) Gretch the Wretch. One reporter wrote that the race was won by an unknown Western housewife, gave all the details but failed to give her name.

The Europeans began to wonder just how high American skiing was regarded in that country after a congratulatory telegram arrived for Gretchen. It was from the Secretary of Commerce under President Harry S. Truman and signed simply, "Ave" (for Averell Harriman who had launched her marriage to Don and her racing career. To his racers, including his own daughter, he wanted to be simply "Ave.")

Always when asked how she attained the fame she replied, "I was fortunate enough to have the support of my husband and of Averell Harriman."[9]

James Laughlin, of New York (and owner of the resort of Alta, Utah), an eloquent ski journalist of that day, wrote:

"If Gretchen had only done well on one day—the combined—we could write it down to chance. But those two consecutive days of greatness and how immeasurably more nerve-tightening must have been the strain for her on the second (day) when every eye and envy was on her, she removed her feat beyond question from the dubious realm of luck to the bright, clear field of things perfectly done by will—of courage, judging and meeting a high risk."[10]

Forty years later as Red Barber was writing memoirs on his long-time broadcasting career (1934 to 1963), he named Gretchen Fraser's Olympic win as one of the 10 most impressive news coverage events he broadcast in his lifetime. She was the only woman athlete on his list and also the only non-baseball event he listed.

Post-Olympic photo of the golden girl from the West. GRETCHEN FRASER
COLLECTION

Here is his rendition:

"In 1948 Edward R. Murrow was in charge of news, special events and sports at CBS. I was asked, as Director of Sports,
to go to St. Moritz to broadcast the Olympics for the Armed
Forces Radio. The broadcast was to be beamed to America at
1 p.m. for CBS Morning News and the CBS Evening News. I
was the only radio man. There was no TV. (Full-scale TV media
coverage of the Games did not begin until the 1960 Olympics.)

"I saw Fraser's first run but due to the 17 minute delay, had to be back at the studio before the other contestants ran the course. I was more upset than Fraser over the delay. I did not know when I left Suvretta if she had won. Just as I was about to go on the air, army officers from the U.S. Armed Forces Radio brought her in and CBS listeners got the first news of America's gold."[11]

Later Barber was informed that Averell Harriman in Washington, D.C. stopped a cabinet meeting to listen to his CBS broadcast on radio and that is how the founder of Sun Valley learned of American skiing's first Olympic gold medal. He had backed the races at Sun Valley because he once said "America was so far behind the Europeans in ski racing talent."[12] Now one of his protégés had changed the tide of history.

Every top wire service of the day used Gretchen Fraser stories: AP, UP, INS, ACME, Hearst. It was as if something like a pick-up team from lower Slovakia came over to the United States and beat the New York Yankees in baseball.

Hearst Newspaper's teenage columnist, Betty Betz summed up the win with the following words which were picked up by the Hearst Service papers in Baltimore, Pittsburg, San Francisco, New York, Chicago and Los Angeles:

"We've broken the ice in snow sport.
Next Olympics we can freeze out the Europeans . . ."

The foreign headlines read:

"Silvio Alvera Leder i Slalom USA's forste gullme dalje"

"Gretchen Fraser takker sin mann for gull-medaljen"

"Olympiamestre Igar: Gretchen Fraser"

The new French magazine L'Equipe printed:

"Surprise Chez les Femmes: l'Américaine Gretchen Fraser spécialiste de descente devient reine du Slalom . . ."

In the space of two days she did 150 interviews and 30 broadcasts. Over 500 cables were received.

Instead of staying in St. Moritz for the celebration parties Gretchen left to fulfill a long standing dream; i.e., to visit her mother's relatives in Norway. Her gold medal was won the day before her parent's 39th wedding anniversary. A few days later was her own 29th birthday (and Don's birthday as well).

On arrival in Scandinavia, the crown prince of Norway invited the American medalist for an audience. This was the same prince Gretchen had skied with on Mount Rainier when he visited America eight years previously. Where a royal audience usually lasts 10 to 15 minutes Gretchen spent about an hour talking of the changes in American skiing since Prince Olav had skied with her (See Chapter II) on Mount Rainier. Nine years later the prince became King Olav of Norway.

Staying long enough to accept the invitation to open the Holmenkollen race, she came back to America on the same boat as Dick Button who had also won a gold medal for the U.S. in the Vth Winter Olympics. He was then 18 years old, skating to Romanian music in a freestyle ice skating performance where the Olympic judges saw him execute the first triple loop jump and first double axle performed in Olympic competition. Previously, he had accumulated the highest scores in the compulsory figures. Clearly, a gold medal performer.

Both athletes sailed from Southampton on February 15 on the Cunard liner, *Queen Elizabeth*. Life would never be the same for either gold medalist again.

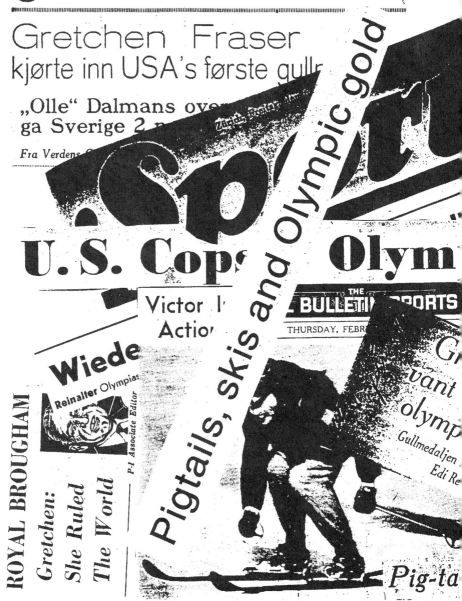

Fredag 6. februar 1948   VERDENS GANG

● Den norske slalåmtekni[

Gretchen Fraser
kjørte inn USA's første gul[

„Olle" Dalmans ov[
ga Sverige 2 [

Fra Verde[

U.S. Cop[Olym

Victor I[
Actio[

THE
BULLETI[[PORTS

THURSDAY, FEBR[

Wiede[

Reinalter Olympia[

ROYAL BROUGHAM

Gretchen:
She Ruled
The World

P-I Associate Editor

Pigtails, Skis and Olympic gold

[G[
vant
olymp

Gullmedaljen
Edi Re[

Pig-ta[

UNITED STATES OLYMPIC COMMITTEE

---VII OLYMPIC WINTER GAMES---
ST. MORITZ, SWITZERLAND ● FEBRUARY-MARCH 1948

- - - GAMES OF THE XIV OLYMPIAD - - -
LONDON, ENGLAND ● JULY-AUGUST 1948

Honorary President
HARRY S. TRUMAN, President of the United States

President Emeritus, GUSTAVUS T. KIRBY

Honorary Vice-Presidents
GEORGE C. MARSHALL, The Secretary of State
KENNETH C. ROYALL, The Secretary of War
JAMES FORRESTAL, The Secretary of Navy

Office of U. S. Olympic Ass'n
BILTMORE HOTEL
43rd St. and Madison Avenue
NEW YORK 17, N. Y.
Tel.: MUrray Hill 5-9328
Cable Address: "AMOLYMPIC"

OFFICERS
President
AVERY BRUNDAGE
10 N. La Salle Street
Chicago 2, Ill.

Vice-President
KENNETH L. WILSON
Hotel Sherman
Chicago 1, Ill.

Secretary
ASA S. BUSHNELL
4 Chambers Terrace
Princeton, N. J.

Treasurer
OWEN V. VAN CAMP
100 W. Monroe Street
Chicago 3, Ill.

OLYMPIC SKI COMMITTEE
Chairman
ALBERT SIGAL
1700 Mills Tower Bldg.
San Francisco, Calif.

Secretary
ARTHUR J. BARTH
3742 West Galena St.
Milwaukee 8, Wis.

FRED BELLMAR
Denver, Colo.

ALEXANDER H. BRIGHT
Boston, Mass.

DARROCH CROOKES
Portland, Oregon

ROGER LANGLEY
Barre, Mass.

C. D. REDDISH
Holaday, Utah

February 5, 1948

Mrs. Gretchen Fraser,
220 W. 26th Street,
Vancouver, Washington

Dear Gretchen:

Nothing could have pleased us any more than the
news which came first last night on the Combined,
and then this morning about the special slalom, and
we both wanted to have this opportunity of telling
you what a swell job you have done, representing
skiing in America. It is a grand performance and
your many friends are sharing with you today, your
happiness.

Our kindest to both you and Don, and surely
hope our ski tracks cross before the winter is out.

Sincerely,

AES:GL

Albert E. Sigal

Après Olympics

W HEN THE *Queen Elizabeth* ocean liner docked in New York an invitation to a party given by Sonja Henie, the Empress of Winter herself, awaited the two Olympians. She threw a wingding celebration for both gold medalists—ice skater, Dick Button, and skier, Gretchen Fraser. Glenn Miller had died in the war, but what was left of his band played until dawn with one of the most popular requests being, "It Happened in Sun Valley."

Sonja had turned her gold medals into millionaire status and became a star on the silver screen. Gretchen did things differently. She had already been in the movies skiing as a double for Sonja in "Thin Ice" (20th Century Fox, 1937) and "Sun Valley Serenade"(20th Century Fox, 1941) and for RKO Pathé during the war in an Otto Lang ski short. **Then** she went on to win the Olympic gold medal. All her films had been done without pay to protect her amateur status.[1]

Mayor William O'Dwyer of New York greeted America's latest sport's heroes at city hall and presented both with scrolls honoring their "great glory to the U.S."

Best of all, for Gretchen, was that Don flew to New York to be there for her arrival. Regally, the pigtails were arranged on top of her head coronet style. She had been gone almost three months and missed Christmas, New Year's Eve,

*Olympic ice skater turned movie star, Sonja Henie (left) and
Gretchen at Sonja's New York party after the '48 Olympics.*
FRASER COLLECTION

Valentine's Day and both her's and Don's birthdays. The "unknown housewife" was now the First Lady of Skiing and returned to a royal homecoming.

They both took an United Airlines Mainliner home instead of the train. From then on it was pride-and-glory time as she traveled throughout the West. In Eugene, Oregon, an Indian tribe honored her with a 3-day powwow naming her "Princess Whitewater."

In Portland there was a banquet for 500 people at the Multnomah Grand Ballroom. Oregon Governor John Hall welcomed her. A 200-pound cake carried by four skiers was presented by the Oregon Winter Sports Association. Someone came up with a novel idea and presented the gold medalist with six gold fish. When golden ski poles were given to her she was so overwhelmed she declared them race trophies to be awarded annually in a Portland race to be called the Golden Poles. Seventeen years later it was still being held in the Northwest with Gretchen on hand to present the perpetual trophy. Now the Northwest had two golden alpine ski races: the Golden Rose and the Golden Poles.

There were silver tea sets and silver candle sticks also presented to her. The latter candlesticks were always to be found polished on her dining room table in Sun Valley to the end of her days.

She reigned as queen of the 15th Annual Daffodil Parade riding in a convertible through Puyallup, Tacoma and Sunger wearing her Olympic uniform. Though she professed to have eaten wonderful food in Switzerland she secretly craved a milk shake and devoured her first one in over three months.

The neighborhood children of Vancouver, Washington were especially excited to welcome her because she had taught many of them to ski. A parade was planned and the schools were let off at 2 p.m. as were city workers.

"Ah home again. I thought I'd never get here. It seems ages since I went away," she was quoted in *The Oregonian* newspaper.

Two U.S. gold medalists from the 1948 Olympics: 18-year-old Dick Button and Gretchen. Note: the 4-leaf clover pin on Gretchen's jacket is explained in this chapter and Chapter VII. FRASER COLLECTION

In an unusual gesture, upon arrival in Vancouver, she requested a stop at the Barnes Veterans Hospital "because they couldn't go to the parade." There one patient, Tommy Thompson, had written a poem about her Olympic win and read it to her. She talked and joked to each patient in the hospital before departing for the city parade.

That unusual hospital stop was the first inkling of the characteristics which the Olympian would exhibit throughout her life to those whom the vicissitudes of good health had taken away some physical ability. She gratefully knew she was physically advantaged. Yet she was humbly touched by those who had to live each day giving a "best effort" try for tasks she took for granted.

All the hoopla in Washington and Oregon was nothing compared to the anticipation of Gretchen's return in Sun Valley, Idaho. She was to arrive to open the annual Harriman Cup events.

An Oregon official gives a royal welcome in Portland. KETCHUM-SUN VALLEY
HISTORICAL MUSEUM COLLECTION

For an arrival reception Tuesday, March 23, 1948, everything was ready. Even the dogs were outfitted in pigtails, made of yellow yarn, to welcome their star. No snowflake was left unturned. A letter dated March 20, 1948, from C.T. Carey to W. P. Rogers, manager of Sun Valley, read:

"Mrs. Fraser will arrive on train 106 and will be met by private auto. On reaching Hailey the driver should signal the telephone operator to call the Sun Valley operator. A blast of whistle will notify all concerned to form in the parade ground in the far west parking lot.

"The order of participants:
Hailey band on foot
Sun Valley Ski School Instructors on foot
Sun Valley Ski Patrol on foot
Victoria carriage with the Frasers
Various hotel personnel on foot or on hayracks.

"The parade will continue through the grounds to Challenger Inn under the arch going east back toward the Lodge. Upon reaching the circle in front of the Lodge the Victoria carriage will fall out of the procession, circle the pool and bring the Frasers to the entrance of the Lodge, where ski instructors and patrol will be in a formation decided upon by Otto Lang. Harl Smith (New York orchestra leader) will have his orchestra in the lobby when she comes in.

"A bouquet will be presented by a small youngster appropriately dressed.

"A puppy, birdcage, and Barsis drawing will be presented at the Harriman Cup banquet . . ."[2]

The puppy, a black Labrador retriever, was a gift of Averell Harriman. Gretchen named the dog, "Saint." He was later replaced by another Labrador which Gretchen called, "Sinner."

Prior to the Olympics the founder of Sun Valley had given the Olympian a gold Tiffany four-leaf clover pin to

Gretchen and Don Fraser with Averell Harriman (middle), circa 1948. Gretchen is wearing her Tiffany good luck pin.
REGIONAL HISTORY DEPT. COMMUNITY LIBRARY, KETCHUM, IDAHO

wear for good luck. After her win the pin was supplemented by a gift of matching gold and sapphire earrings.

(Both these cherished possessions figure prominently in the depiction of her life many years later. See Chapter VII)

World-wide the honors continued to pour in. The Ski Club of Great Britain conferred upon her the Pery Medal , the Fédération Francaise de Ski and the Norwegian government also gave her awards. She was named Woman Athlete of the Year by the National Press Club. The National Ski Association presented her the American Ski Trophy. The USSA gave her the 1948 Beck International Award. It took, however, until 1960 for her to be inducted as the 21st member of the National Ski Hall of Fame.

The unveiling of the memorial honoring 100 years of St. Moritz skiing and their two Olympics. Gretchen as invited guest is eighth from left in the upper row. KETCHUM-SUN VALLEY HISTORICAL MUSEUM COLLECTION

Allen Adler, chairman of the National Ski Hall of Fame selection committee who had seen his share of famous skiers remarked on Gretchen: " She was a warm friendly person always signing off her letters with one word, 'affectionately.' Too few of her around any more."

Doctor Merrit Stiles, president at that time of the United States Ski Educational Foundation, gave the Ski Hall of Fame plaque to Gretchen at a Warren Miller ski show in Portland, November 7, 1961. Her husband and 12-year-old son, Bill, were there.

For the event a stainless steel Rolex watch commemorating her Olympic win was presented supplementing a gold Rolex she was given by the company twelve years previously.

Averell Harriman and his protégé at Sun Valley after her gold.

She attended many succeeding Olympics and was invited as the only American honoree when St. Moritz celebrated its 100th birthday as a winter resort. When she returned to St. Moritz she was accompanied this time by her husband. St. Moritz held many happy memories for the Olympian, but there was a sad note too on her return. On the second day of the celebration, the resort dedicated a monument to American ski

Wally Huffman, general manager of Sun Valley, and Gretchen inaugurate a
new run called "Gretchen's Gold" in 1978. It was thirty years after her
historic Olympic achievement. Gretchen was 59 years old at the time.
PHOTO BY LARRY HILL FROM KETCHUM-SUN VALLEY HISTORICAL MUSEUM COLLECTION

The heated swimming pool of Sun Valley Inn, Sun Valley Lodge and Harriman Cottage with a backdrop of Baldy runs, the year Seattle Ridge was developed. An arrow points to the run, Gretchen's Gold.
SUN VALLEY COMPANY

racer, Buddy Werner and German ski racer Barbi Henneberger. The previous spring both were killed in an avalanche while being filmed for a ski movie in the Saluver Valley not far from the site of Gretchen's Olympic victory.

The Frasers another time took their son and his wife, Linda, with them to Switzerland for a nostalgic tour. Gretchen tried to show them the plaque with the names of the gold medal winners from the 1928 and the 1948 Winter Olympics engraved on it. Alas, the snow was so deep that year it covered the place on the plaque where her name was recorded for history.

Years later in the U. S. at a conference of six western governors in Telluride, Colorado, she was presented the Pioneers of Skiing award for her contribution to the sport of skiing. Subsequent to talks she gave as an inspirational speaker she received many honors from university and individual groups. To keep things in perspective she hung some of her honors in the utility room of her home.

In the '70s when the Seattle Ridge area of Sun Valley's Baldy mountain was developed, the run closest to the Number 12 lift was named "Gretchen's Gold."

When Sun Valley Lodge was remodeled in 1986 Gretchen gave her Olympic gold medal (made of six ounces of pure gold in 1948) to be displayed in the lobby. There it resided in a special glass case until it mysteriously disappeared one day a few years later.

Rewards were offered, clues sought to its disappearance, posters put up in local post offices, but it remained missing. At first Gretchen thought it had been taken out of its glass case by Sun Valley Company for some use, but on inquiring, it could not be accounted for. The lock was not broken, nor the hinges of the case tampered. Gretchen was heartbroken as were all at Sun Valley. Then over a month later it suddenly reappeared in a box mailed without a return address. An explanation for the short disappearance has never been given.

Perhaps even thieves were charmed into repentance by the woman who had quietly made her mark in the small mountain community.

 WELCOME HOME, GRETCHEN

Queen of World's Women Skiers Arrived Yesterday In Her Old Home Town

SIX

Passing the Torch

ALMOST AT THE FINISH LINE of her 1948 gold medal victory, Gretchen announced she was going to retire from racing.

"I have a husband I haven't seen in three months and in the future I prefer a family life. I'm happily married. You can't be that and go on racing. I am convinced you can't have both," she told an AP reporter.

By the next December Donald William, Jr., was born weighing 9 lbs, 4 oz. Gretchen's friend, Kathleen Harriman Mortimer, was asked to be his godmother. Gretchen reciprocated for a son of Kathleen's born about a year later.

Had she not won the Olympic medals she may possibly have been content to be Mrs. Donald W. Fraser of 7617 East Maple Avenue in a house near the outskirts of Vancouver, Washington on a little wooded area with panoramic views of Oregon's Mount Hood and of Mount Adams in Washington state. The gold medal changed all that. She now belonged to the people. Demands for her time poured in and she accepted the challenge gracious as always.

On March 29, 1948, she signed a three year contract for a position as Public Relations Assistant for the Union Pacific resort of Sun Valley. The pay was $500/month plus expenses and a pass on the railroad. In addition all endorsements were allowed as long as the product associated her name with Sun Valley.

Kathleen and Gretchen with their children. Gretchen is on the right with son, Donald William Jr., standing in front of her. FRASER COLLECTION

Lux soap wanted Gretchen's endorsement but wouldn't agree to the Sun Valley tie-in. No deal was signed. Jantzen sweaters agreed to Sun Valley's name and Gretchen's name both, giving her a $1,000 contract and all the Jantzen pants and sweaters she wanted. Wheaties put her on its cereal boxes from 1948 to 1953 promoting the "breakfast of champions." Charlie Bell, head of Wheaties, wanted some American on his cereal boxes to show Europeans that Americans could ski. She was ideal even though Averell Harriman always said to her that steak was the best day's start for an athlete. No one ever asked her what she really did eat.

(In negotiating the first endorsement contracts for a winning ski athlete, Steve Hannegan with his promotional expertise, unknowingly set a prosperous stage for future ski champions. By 1984 endorsements for winning skiers were so lucrative that Sarajevo's downhill gold medalist, Bill Johnson of the U.S., had only to answer a reporter's question of: "What does the win mean to you?" with his famous one word sentence: "Millions.")

Gretchen's contract with Sun Valley meant she was to be available for assignments when called upon. It was intended to use her promotional value not only for Sun Valley winter but spring, summer, and fall seasons too.

In 1950 Hannegan decided that Gretchen should go on a 6-week 21-city tour on behalf of the U.S. Ski Team. He reasoned that the sports world always is interested in champions but seldom does it have one who possesses what Gretchen had—sportsmanship and personality. A Union Pacific train sped across the country to raise funds for the team but at the same time it greatly promoted Sun Valley. Her son was only 18 months old at the time so she hired a nursemaid to take care of him.

The Union Pacific got its money's worth as she gave 26 talks in 21 cities before 16,000 people plus charmed the guests at 57 lunches, cocktail parties and dinners.

The Fraser family, circa 1960. A FRAMED PICTURE THAT HUNG IN THEIR HOME

Gretchen (right) and Frances Scully, a popular Hollywood reporter on Los Angeles radio KECA, 1950, discuss Sun Valley.
STEVE HANNEGAN & ASSOC.

In Los Angeles alone she had lunch with some of the city's sports editors and generated stories in the following newspapers, the impressive magnitude of which was proudly reported[1] by Hannegan and Associates to the Union Pacific office:

Los Angeles Times (circulation 396,717)
Los Angeles Examiner (361,904)
Herald Express (369,261)
The Mirror (195,000)

Terse word-slugging editors familiar with rugged, leathery athletes of more muscular proportions were simply bowled over by the petite, 5 ft. 4 inch, 115-pound medalist who showed up for lunch in a white hat and gloves.

In his column, "Between the Sports's Lines" for the *Sacramento* (CA) *Union*, Wilbur Adams, who hated snow and any

At the Southern California Press Club with leading sports writers and editors, 1950. Gretchen in middle wearing white hat, Paul Zimmerman (at Gretchen's left), sports editor of the LOS ANGELES TIMES *and Mrs. Ethel Van de Grift, ski columnist for the* TIMES. *Al Santoro, sports editor of the* LOS ANGELES EXAMINER.
STEVE HANNEGAN & ASSOC.

weather associated with it, took one look at her and typed out a story with the lead: "I think I'll take up skiing . . ."

Although the purpose of the tour was to raise money for the upcoming FIS team in Aspen (1950) and the Olympic team (1952), in interviews of 13 radio broadcasts and seven telecasts she stood for Sun Valley while the Union Pacific railroad was mentioned often. In one of her letters to Steve Hannegan she confided she was having a hard time getting television to mention the Union Pacific but they never balked at mentioning Sun Valley.

Sometimes she shared the program with John Jay who had been official cinematographer at the 1948 Olympics. Wherever his film was shown, the lobby of the theater also had posters displayed of Sun Valley resort.

In addition she appeared for four hours on given days during well-advertised, three-day promotions at Bloomingdale's in New York and Marshall Field in Chicago plus numerous ski shops. Gretchen asked $100 per appearance at the department stores with 100%, of all money raised, going to America's ski team. The department store appearances were her idea. Funds started pouring in for U.S. skiing.

Audiences from coast to coast were taken with her modesty, charm and poise. Not once did she refuse to accept an engagement. No appointment was ever missed in the 45-day tour, much to the amazement of Hannegan who had previously dealt mostly with demanding prima donna celebrities.

The public relations impresario who had put Miami Beach on the map was getting his first taste of athletic dedication.

If Hannegan had ever listened to Gretchen talk to a group of Girl Scouts he would not have been so amazed. She once told a group of Scouts that discipline is one of the most important things in life. "If you can not discipline yourself you'll never accomplish your goals," she told them.

Everywhere she went she became skiing good-will ambassador. The U.S. Ski Team was $15,000 richer which was almost $1/_3$ their budget. Those were the days when a coke cost 5 cents; bread cost 25 cents a loaf and an elegantly served six course meal at the Sun Valley Lodge set skiers back under $4.00.

If a racer came up to her asking advice she replied, "I think I could stay calm in a tornado. If you can lick tension and anxiety you have a head start over the field. You don't make mistakes."[2] (That may explain her dead-pan cool for the winning Olympic run after the long delay at the start gate.)

A letter went out at the end of the tour praising Gretchen. It read:

"Without 100% co-operation, tremendous vitality and unusual composure under trying conditions, the tour could not have had such outstanding success."

Gretchen took the praise in stride.

"My father always said: 'When you partake of a sport and it gives you something, you give something back to it.'"

All along the way, people kept asking her where her pigtails were. Gretchen laughed and answered,

"Pigtails, pigtails, pigtails! In the parade at Sun Valley every horse and dog wore pigtails and in Vancouver half the girls wore their hair that way. I got so sick of pigtails by springtime I had my hair cut."

On the heels of the successful fund-raising tour, America's ski race officials prepared for the 1952 Winter Olympics in Oslo with gusto. The woman who had retired victoriously from racing saying, "I'm just not competitive by nature," still was not far from the race courses. She was appointed team manager for the 1952 U.S. Women's Alpine Olympic Team. Kathleen Mortimer was chairman of the clothing committee. The diplomat's daughter rounded up travel and training uniforms, all generously donated by American manufacturers, snagging full page spreads in fashion magazines.

The two ex-racers worked well together. They had been friends since Gretchen came to her first Harriman Cup race in 1938, more than a decade before. They were both married now, both mothers but their ties to the ski racers of America remained.

Gretchen had known Bing Crosby from when he entertained the troops during the war at Sun Valley so she persuaded him to send over a couple hundred cartons of orange juice from the Minute Maid company he owned. Fruit juice was scarce in Norway.

Duty driven, Gretchen as team manager, filed perceptive reports of the women's race training progress. They left January 2 at 4:00 in the afternoon by air from New York to Zurich—a 15-hour flight. It took almost a month's less travel time than it had four years previously for the '48 Olympics.

Movie star Van Johnson shows Gretchen the script of the movie "The Dutchess of Idaho," while filming at Sun Valley in 1950.
FROM SCRAPBOOK

Few members of the team had ever flown across the Atlantic, including Gretchen.

"I recommend air travel for future teams," she wrote as the team proceeded to the mountains on an itinerary carefully planned during the summer by Cortland "Corty" Hill, Chair-

Team manager Gretchen congratulates Andrea Mead at the 1952 Olympics. U.S. SKI HALL OF FAME

man of the U.S. Olympic Ski Committee, and Alice Kiaer. The budget was now $52,000 for the team.

Hopes for more gold ran high and Andrea "Andy" Mead Lawrence of Pico Peak, Vermont—now 19 years old and married to team mate, Dave Lawrence—did not disappoint anyone. By now the special slalom event was replaced by the giant slalom, and there were medals for downhill, slalom and giant slalom. The combined no longer was calculated. Andy won two gold medals in impressive wins in both giant slalom and slalom. She placed 17th in the downhill and might have earned another medal but the scoring for the combined had been dropped.

Team manager Gretchen wrote in her report that Andy's seasoning in Europe had paid off. From then on American ski racers of note were given the opportunity to go to European competitions. The country was no longer an isolationist nation. The war, which the country had tried to stay out of for so long, had taught the nation that much.

Gretchen did have her woes with the women's team though. Team member Susie Harris (Rytting) was found to be pregnant and had to be sent home. Katy Rodolph of the U.S. womens' alpine team was trying to keep secret her marriage to Keith Wegemann on the U. S. jumping team, as he was a military flier and officially prohibited from marriage.

A meeting was called by Corty Hill, head of the U. S. Olympic Ski Committee.[3] Gretchen as women's team manager was there, along U.S. Cross country coach, Leif Odmark, and other American ski officials. The couple was confronted and both Katy and Keith admitted they had been secretly married. By the time the press got wind of the predicaments of Susie, Katy and Keith, the Olympics were in full swing and the games went on without embarrassment to anyone. The U.S. Olympic Committee, in a letter to Gretchen, praised her for her discrete handling of the delicate situations.

The post-Olympic period for Gretchen lasted her whole life, not just to the next Olympics. She was always interested in the competitors. Thus she became involved in the formative years of the American Athletic Academy[4] which assists national caliber athletes in completing their education, in career counseling and placement. Many times she voiced the opinion that international competition engenders a tunnel vision in athletes who must devote all their attention to their skills and need help to regain a sense of balance in their affairs after competition.

Through the years she saw many changes in the U.S. Ski Team policies, not the least being that by 1968 $350,000 was raised to send the team to the Olympics in Grenoble, France. Though her 1948 women's team arrived at the Olympics with not enough funds for a coach, by 1996 the Women's U. S. Ski Team hired a head coach, three coaches for downhill and super-G, another two for slalom and giant slalom, plus an equipment coordinator, and a physiotherapist. Those were just the staff positions for the women. The men's team had more.

Also by the '90s it became increasingly impossible for amateur American athletes to compete with the Europeans who were essentially paid professionals in Olympic competition. Gretchen's opinion was sought out. Without a trace of bitterness at the program to present cash stipends of $15,000, $10,000 and $5,000 respectively to American 1st, 2nd and 3rd finishers in the 1994 Lillehammer Olympics she replied,

"My that sounds good. I have no complaints. At least I got my way paid to St. Moritz unlike Don who worked his way to the Olympics on a freighter. That's just the way the times were."

SEVEN

Gretchen's Gifts

F AME, IN ALL WALKS OF LIFE, sometimes creates havoc on marriages. To a love affair less solidly blessed than Gretchen's and Don's, where they shared the slopes that produced the fame and fortune, life at the summit might have taken its toll.

During the Olympics, Gretchen had skied with a prince (the prince of Liechtenstein), been feted by another prince (Crown Prince Olav of Norway) and chauffeured by the owner of a Rolls Royce (Charles de Chateau of Belgium). (See Chapter IV) Those things alone, not to mention the world accolades for winning America's first Olympic gold medal in skiing, would have swelled the head of most 28-year olds on their first trip to Europe.

Not Mrs. Donald W. Fraser. Life was never the same for Gretchen after the Olympics; but the person was the same.

She humbly realized she was physically advantaged but her heart forever went out to those whose physical ability had been diminished.

The Flying Outriggers

SHORTLY AFTER HER 1948 TRIUMPH she resumed her role as a volunteer for the causes of the handicapped. She had seen the war victims first hand and could never forget them. For 27 years she sat on the board of the Oregon Institute of Rehabilitation. At Madigan Convalescent Hospital in Fort Lewis, Washington, she taught riding and swimming in rehabilitation clinics and founded The Flying Outriggers, a club for amputee skiers.

She often spoke of how she noticed that those who were complainers never seemed to get along in their recovery as well as did those who honestly kept trying, and were proud of their successes, no matter how minor they seemed.

One time in later years at Sun Valley she was watching an amputee ski and went up to him to tell him how much she was admiring his skiing ability. He said, "You may have forgotten but you started me skiing 18 years ago."[1]

Gretchen always referred to that incident as her most rewarding experience.

Equestrian Causes

ALWAYS WELL MANNERED she fought for her causes with grace—the same warm, friendly way she exhibited in ski competitions. As a leading equestrian in the Pacific Northwest she helped open the doors to women's participation in the Olympic equestrian events—the 3-day riding event and stadium jumping event which were formerly military status and strictly the province of male riders. For six years she served on the U.S. Equestrian board. She rode hunters and jumpers. On horses named "Victory Man" and "Briarcrest" she took the Columbia Hunt horse shows with the same deftness exhibited in the winter Olympics.

Even after her Olympic win she continued in horse competitions until one time loading a horse into its trailer she became tangled in a rope and suffered severe neck injuries.

As multi-faceted as her interests were, she was equally talented in them.

At Home on Skis or Saddle

Gretchen Fraser, the U. S. Olympics ski ace, will display her riding skill at Columbia Hunt club's Horseman's Holiday show on Sunday, August 24, at Hayden island. The comely slats queen is pictured above with her mount, Victory Man.

Gretchen the equestrienne. THE OREGONIAN

*The founder of Sun Valley and his racer, Gretchen, wearing the
diamond Harriman race pin. The pin was awarded to those who
completed a run down Baldy Mt. under a set time. Gretchen was one
of the first women to receive the diamond Harriman.*
KETCHUM-SUN VALLEY HISTORICAL MUSEUM COLLECTION

Olympic ski medalist in flight gear with T-33 jet. Circa 1965.
KETCHUM-SUN VALLEY HISTORICAL MUSEUM COLLECTION

The Ninety Nines

SINCE DON WAS A PILOT she took up flying mostly for him. When she found herself an "aviation widow" she rounded up other wives of pilots in Vancouver and made up a ground school class to study navigation and weather. She soloed before her Olympics but did not get her wings as a private pilot until 1958, ten years later.

At a Sun Valley Ski Club Reunion (from left): Averell Harriman, Lowell Thomas and Friedl Pfeifer tell tales at the Ram Restaurant in Sun Valley. The partial face of ex-racer Hannah Locke Carter is in the lower left. Circa 1970. SUN VALLEY NEWS BUREAU

During this time Don's petroleum business, now under the name Don Fraser Co., continued to prosper under his leadership. He was financially able to purchase a Beechcraft airplane for his thriving business.

A year later both Don and Gretchen flew with Lowell Thomas to the Polar Ice Cap to participate in the skiing sequences for his "High Adventure" series on TV. Gretchen was the first woman there and camped out like the rest.

The Fraser's son, Donald William Jr. who was called "Bill," always knew his parents were famous, he said, because people

like Lowell Thomas were often at their home. Lowell Thomas
was Don's idol.[2] Their son was 11 years old at the time of that
polar trip to Juneau, Alaska and beyond. His most vivid rec-
ollection of it was seeing photos of his mother, amid all the
snow and ice, attired in a bra-like halter soaking up the sun.

Gretchen logged over 3,000 hours in multi-engine craft of
more than a dozen different types. "Few men compare with
her as a pilot," said Myles Ruggonberg, her civil aeronautic
administration check pilot. When Art Linkletter had her on
his TV show she met jet test pilot, Chuck Yeager, which re-
sulted in flying jets as a co-pilot with him. Later she was inducted into the Boise chapter of The Ninety Nines, Inc.—an
elite international women pilot's association.

Sometimes, in the exuberance of hero worship, people erroneously attribute exaggerations of glory—more than what ac-
tually took place. Many write-ups conferred the winning
of the Powder Puff Derby to Gretchen. Yet a check of the
roster of Derby winners does not contain her name. So I con-
tacted Gene Nora Jessen, a past president of the Idaho Ninety
Nines.

"Gretchen didn't know how the rumor of the Derby win
started and it really embarrassed her," said Jessen. "Many
people of great athletic ability make good pilots. So Gretchen's
expertise as a pilot would not be unusual," continued Jessen,
"but she never won that famous long distance women's aviation race."[3]

Gretchen had two open-chest surgeries in the '70s and '80s,
resulting in six coronary artery bypasses that curtailed her flying in later life.

Even when the Olympian no longer renewed her aviation
medical, due to debilitating heart disease, she made light of her
plight. Jessen, writing in the *99 News* international magazine
wrote her most vivid picture of Gretchen:

"The last time I saw her she came into the FBO (field base
operator where airplanes gas up and repairs are made) *in a*

Citation (the model name for a twin-engine jet airplane made by Cessna) *with an optimistic report saying, 'No more bypasses, but I can still ski.' "*

The words in parenthesis were not in Jessen's obituary write-up of Gretchen for the 99 *News.* They are added here for readers not familiar with aviation lingo. Though the Olympian did not pilot a plane in later years, she was still an often-requested passenger because of her knowledge of flying.

When Gretchen joined The Ninety Nines, the Idaho chapter was so enamored by her that they asked her for a replica of her Winter Olympic gold medal for display in the international headquarters for the organization. That is how Winter Olympic ski memorabilia came to be in the unlikely place of The Ninety Nines Resource Center in Oklahoma City, Oklahoma.

Retirement

THE FRASERS RETIRED TO SUN VALLEY from the petroleum products distributorship, when Sun Valley Co. built the Villager condos in 1968. They were 55 and 49 years old, respectively and had been married for over 30 years. They had worked hard. Don's Beechcraft airplane which he piloted moved with them. They wanted to retire to the rewards that Sun Valley living could provide for them.

Their son now was in his twenties and in the Army Air Force serving in Vietnam. The knowledge of airplanes had been passed on from his parents. Upon returning from Vietnam he settled in Woodinville, Washington.

Living again back in Sun Valley, Gretchen and Don resumed their youth despite medical problems encountered by each.

A few years into retirement Don was hospitalized with rheumatoid arthritis. Then later that same year he was resuscitated with electric shock after cardiac arrest, spending 10 days in intensive care

In 1970 Averell Harriman at 78 years of age takes to the slopes again. SUN VALLEY NEWS BUREAU UNDER JANSS CORP.

afterwards. But he bounced back to become an observer on the 1979 Annapurna III expedition to Nepal climbing to 19,000 feet.

After their move back to Sun Valley they had almost a quarter of a century to hike, fly, ski, hunt, fish, golf, all the time continuing to give back to the community the richness it had provided them.

In papers discovered after Gretchen's death was a note written in her careful handwriting (with the ts always crossed in a slant). It was a preliminary for a speech she was asked to give, reading:

"If you accept and take advantages offered by a community or country you give of volunteer time and money in return for that privilege. Also if you criticize a person or project or law, you must also offer a constructive criticism and where possible do something about it."

Gretchen and Kathleen have tea inside Harriman cottage in front of the view window. Circa 1970.

That explains the characteristic gifts which Gretchen exhibited throughout her days. When called upon to lend her famous presence to Valley causes she quickly accepted. To those who found tragedy suddenly thrust upon them, her heart would seem to break and they would be touched by her in some way. To anyone who asked for help, she tried to give from the depths of her soul. On a one on one basis she made everyone she met feel special and even precious.

Some examples:

The Special Olympics

IN 1976 A SUN VALLEY RESIDENT, Shirley Brashears with a Down's syndrome child, was asked to start an Idaho Special Olympics for people of mental retardation. She needed a guiding light and called upon Gretchen to be honorary chairman. She hesitated to ask someone whose sports credentials were so impressive, yet she knew the value of sports to build self esteem and gain social skills for mentally challenged children. She asked.

Gretchen Fraser Meets the Challenges of 1986

Gretchen Fraser receives the Special Olympics award from Arnold Schwarzenegger and Frank Gifford in New York City, Sept. 12.

Gretchen accepted and took up the cause. She was rewarded with the International Coach of the Year award for the Special Olympics.

Without any special skills dealing with such she reasoned—as she had with the amputees in Utah and Oregon—using one thought: There must be a way.

Most of all she showed that she cared. She took a particular interest in the Brashears' son. "To Gretchen he was special and always precious," said Mrs. Brashears.

The Frasers had just arrived home from traveling in Scandinavia and Russia with Dr. John and Jean Moritz of Sun Valley when word was received that Gretchen was to receive the Special Olympics Coach of the Year award at the United Nations building in New York. She alighted in Sun Valley for one day only and then flew to New York to receive the award at a large luncheon.

There she ran into an old friend who often visited Sun Valley, Eunice Kennedy Shriver, who started the Special Olympics in 1968. By the '90s there were more than 250,000 qualified Special Olympic coaches around the world who train over 1 million athletes in 150 countries for at least eight weeks before each sports competition held for people with mental retardation.

(The lucite book ends which were presented to the Coach of the Year by Arnold Schwarzenegger and Frank Gifford that day are in the Sun Valley-Ketchum Ski and Heritage Museum.)

When the honored coach returned to Sun Valley she learned her sternum had not healed properly from a previous open heart surgery. On September 29 that same year she underwent a bone graft.

The Avalanche

IN NOVEMBER, 1972 the Frasers went to Nepal with Bill and Anne Janss. Two months later Anne Janss was dead. She died in a snow avalanche while helicopter skiing on Malcomb Ridge seven miles north of Sun Valley on January 22, 1973.

A group, of 11 resort guests and five certified mountain guides, was helicopter skiing its second run of the day when a snow wall broke loose 75 feet above four members of the party. Sam and Peggy Grossman plus Serge Gagarin were knocked

Averell Harriman returns to Sun Valley after a long absence. Mrs. Anne Janss escorts him on arrival at Hailey airport under crossed ski poles. Circa 1970. THE EVENING OUTLOOK, SANTA MONICA

half a mile down the mountainside and not seriously injured. The body of Mrs. Janss was found 50 feet beyond the other three. She was dead under two feet of snow, her face covered with an inch of ice.

Only a couple of nights before they had all been dancing in the Lodge to the music of Hap Miller as he played, "It Happened in Sun Valley" for another Sun Valley Ski Club reunion. In the early morning hours Bill took off for Salt Lake City on business and Anne went skiing for her last time.

Bill Janss recalled, years later, that it was Don and Gretchen who came by his house and got him to re-enter the world after that by enticing him to get out on a short cross country ski trek. "They always seemed so attuned to helping others and knew just how to do it," he said.

Middle age crisis: Prominent former alpine ski racers (from left), Dick Durrance, Hannah Locke Carter, Miggs Durrance, Kathleen Harriman, Gretchen Fraser, Don Fraser and unidentified man take up the cross-country craze of 1970s. LEIF ODMARK COLLECTION

Bill recovered and later married widow Glenn Candy Cooper whose daughter, Christin, was destined to win a silver Olympic alpine ski medal in the Sarajevo Olympics of 1984.

THERE ARE MANY UNTOLD other stories of the good that Gretchen did. Two that touched me immensely are related on the following pages. They are written in a more personal tone, because that is how they affected me.

Three Presents for Muffy

THERE ARE PEOPLE LIVING in coastal lowlands who may never again leave a successive pair of footprints along a beach as the tide is running out. There are people skiing in the mountain highlands who may never again leave their boot prints in the new fallen snow of a thousand winter storms. They, however, never fail to make an impression, wherever they go.

Muffy Davis is one of them. I found her on top of Sun Valley's Bald Mountain on a mid-winter day when the thermometer was hovering in the single digits. The date: February,1996. I followed her down to the bottom of Warm Springs.

Seven years previously, while in high school, Muffy was a promising young Sun Valley racer so good that she was receiving short congratulation letters from Gretchen Fraser, whom she had never met. Gretchen kept writing how proud she was of the young Sun Valley competitor's race results. She felt she was headed places.

Then in 1989, Muffy was paralyzed following a ski training accident on Baldy.

When she was in the hospital afterwards, Gretchen was so deeply moved by the young racer's plight that she gave the girl's father (a doctor at the hospital) one of her most treasured gifts to give Muffy.

The Frasers had been in a car accident the day after Muffy's accident and had come to the hospital for x-rays. Gretchen, by then, had word of the extent of Muffy's injuries and brought with her the Tiffany gold four-leaf clover pin (see Chapter V) which Averell Harriman had given his protégé back in 1948 to bring her luck in the Olympics. Gretchen said she wanted the talented racer, now a paraplegic, to have it and the same good fortune she had.

Muffy reported that Gretchen, as their friendship grew, later gave her the matching sapphire earrings Harriman had given her after she brought back America's first Olympic alpine ski medals.

"I am sure my father would have approved of Gretchen's thoughtful gift," said Kathleen Harriman to the Wood River Valley news reporters as word of the golden gifts of Gretchen spread to her. (Her famous father, the founder of Sun Valley, had died a few years previously).

As time went on Muffy, still a paraplegic, graduated from high school. Gretchen, still in touch, then presented her with the amethyst and gold link bracelet her own parents had given her upon high school graduation in Tacoma.

Five years after her accident as the 1994 Olympics were about to begin. Muffy wrote a perceptive letter sharing the effect of the Frasers on her. The tiny Wood River Valley was left with the indelible feeling that there were some people who knew what competition—the winning and the losing—were all about.

These are Muffy's words:

"We've all been witness to some of the worst effects of competitive athletics over the past few weeks (referring to the Tonya Harding incident which attempted to incapacitate skater Nancy Kerrigan). This really contrasts so much with those values manifest in the life of other outstanding athletes that it makes one

Gretchen wears the gold Tiffany four-leaf clover pin given her by
Averell Harriman for good luck.

reconsider where our emphasis should be placed as we mold the lives of our young. Don Fraser was half of a partnership of two premier athletes who will long be remembered for their graciousness and humanity **in spite of** *rather than* **because of** *their athletic prowess. We never really knew Don or Gretchen as athletes, only as wonderful, supportive people. Their athletic careers magnified their status but did not define their beings... Gretchen's Gold (the ski run) may have been named for her Olympic medal, but it is equally appropriate for her heart and soul... equal measures of athleticism and humanism.... They have given us an ideal to try to attain."*[4]

Muffy graduated from Stanford University in 1995—still paralyzed.

But that is not the end of her story.

Racing was in her bloodstream. She never gave up that she would one day race again. The 1994 Olympics, to which she had once aspired to be in, were concluded without her. But during the 1995–96 ski season Muffy entered a national race. It was the Winter Park Handicap Nationals in Colorado.

When I met Muffy in February, 1996 it was just after her return home to Sun Valley from that race. There at the bottom of Warm Springs—where Sun Valley racers ever since 1939 had asked the same question—people were repeating the racer's mantra:

"How'd ya do in the race"?

"Oh, I'm improving," she replied with a laugh.

We rode the Greyhawk lift together as she maneuvered her mono-ski rigged chair deftly on and off the high-speed quad lift with more ease than the snowboarder who was riding with us. Her arms, which were not paralyzed, help propel her down the slopes aided by outrigger ski tips hinged on poles.

"Gretchen gave so much," said Muffy while riding the chairlift. "I hope I can inspire someone like Gretchen did."

I skied behind her down to a place on lower Hemingway run where some gates had been set up for training. She was fast and cool. I was whole and humbled.

Two decades later Gretchen Fraser manager of the 1952 women's Olympic ski team and Leif Odmark, who was the 1952 men's cross country coach hold a reunion on the slopes. Circa 1972. LEIF ODMARK COLLECTION

An inspiration? To me she had already become one. Someone named Gretchen had taught her how to never give up—even when things seemed almost impossible to do.

Two Gifts to a Journalist

In many cases journalists, too, received the generosity of Gretchen's time. Though she had just returned from a hospital treatment for her cancer she came to a Sun Valley Lodge banquet for the United States Ski Writers Association in 1966 during their annual meeting there. She chatted with the ski writing press as if nothing were wrong. She had no complaints of her cancer, not mentioning it.

On an individual basis, twice I was helped on assignments by Gretchen. The first time was 1969 when the Sunday magazine of the *Los Angeles Times* wanted an article on W. Averell Harriman who was at the height of his diplomatic career. Gretchen offered a tip no one else would have thought to give me, as I prepared to interview the famous diplomat.

"Sit on his right side because he is deaf in his left ear," she advised.

As a result all one afternoon in the Georgetown, Virginia, mansion of the distinguished diplomat he talked of Sun Valley and its early days and a fledgling journalist got an interview on a part of Harriman few people knew at the time.[5] "I will tell you the genesis of Sun Valley . . . ," he began while Queen Elizabeth, from a silver picture frame on the piano looked on in awe; Bobby Kennedy smiled on us from his portrait on the mantle; and Roosevelt, Churchill and Stalin at Yalta stared in amazement from their place on the bookshelf.

Harriman was inducted into the U.S. Ski Hall of Fame that year.

Twenty-two years later I was doing a story for *Snow Country* magazine on Virginia Hill, gangster Bugsy Siegel's girl friend. The movie "Bugsy" had just come out staring Annette Bening and Warren Beatty. The film came to an abrupt end when Bugsy was shot to death. An epilogue had just one sentence: Virginia Hill died in Austria.

The gist of my article was to verify the legend I had heard often around Sun Valley that Virginia Hill had come to the resort after the gangster was shot to death. She arrived tipping everyone with $100 bills from a shoe box and left with her private ski instructor, Hans Hauser, who was the first head of the ski school.

The editor of the magazine would settle for nothing less than a photo of Hill taken at Sun Valley to prove she had truly been there.

Two weeks in the resort searching the usual resources for such a photo yielded nothing. Finally, Bebe Hammerle, the widow of an early-day ski instructor, provided a photo from a long forgotten scrap book, but then the editor wanted more.

Assignment completed? No.

John Fry, who was editor of *Snow Country* at the time, had shown the article, close-to-deadline stage, to some editors of the *New York Times* which owned the magazine. Between them they decided they wanted me to find the son (born 40 years before) from the marriage of the ski instructor and the gangster's moll. Both Hans and Virginia had died under mysterious circumstances in Austria some years before and no one at Sun Valley even knew the offspring's name as the parents had fled the country shortly after their elopement.

Where to start? I called Gretchen for the phone number in Austria of Hans Hauser's brother, Max, who I knew had been a ski instructor at Sun Valley before the war.

Gretchen had just thrown her old telephone book in the trash can after copying some numbers into a new book. She knew Max Hauser too had died so his entry was not copied to her new book. Yet—totally uncalled for—she went to her trash cans and rummaged through to come up with her old phone book containing an Austrian phone number. This eventually led to the son, Peter Hauser, found growing grapes in Italy.

Thus Gretchen through her kindness and "night-time garbage can caper", provided the crux of the story which appeared titled "'Bugsy': The Rest of the Story," in the October 1992 *Snow Country* magazine.[6]

The movie, "Bugsy," won two Academy Awards in 1991 (costume design plus art direction and set decoration) but to skiers the story of what happened after Hollywood proclaimed, "The End" is a far more intriguing tale.

PERHAPS GRETCHEN'S GREATEST GIFT was that she truly enoyed people. She seemed equally at home whether sharing a sandwich out of a knapsack or a meal at her dining room table laden with crystal and silver.

Her interests were as varied as her friends. She laughed at

some of the many titles she acquired in her lifetime. One was that of: "The Only Woman to Go Bird Hunting With Lipstick."

Invited to go hunting with 10 men, one morning she was up early. The dogs which she loved to watch working, were out ahead. As she walked along admiring the scenery one of the dogs flushed a covey of partridge. Being one of only two women on the trip she was suddenly given the honor of the first shot.

Fumbling in her pocket for her shells she made a mistake and grabbed her lipstick. Of course she jammed her gun with it. Thus the dubious title.

Her long-time friend, Anita Gray, who moved to Sun Valley in 1948 after the war, tells of the early days in Sun Valley, a time when skiers made their own après ski.

"Gretchen loved to play Charades," Anita said. "There just was not much to do at night if you did not drink or gamble. Don was not as enthusiastic but he played the game to please Gretchen. He wasn't much for horses either but he went on rides for the same reason."

That was the story of their life, they lived for each other.

The two racers met and fell in love when she was a University of Puget Sound co-ed and the love affair lasted a lifetime.

To tell the story of Gretchen is to pen a love story in addition to writing of the legacy she left after winning America's first Olympic gold medal in skiing.

Astrology buffs would make much over the fact that Don and Gretchen shared the same birth day. To those who go by the signs of the zodiac they were both born under the sign of Aquarius. Take it for what it is worth.

Friends, oftentimes, like to joke that knowing the Frasers saved them money. Because Gretchen and Don shared the same birth date (February ll), they only had to pay for one postage stamp to wish both of them "Happy Birthday." Wittily both Don and Gretchen proclaimed that their long happy marriage was because they never forgot when their spouse's birthday was.

In later years their happiest times were at the Nature Conservancy of Idaho, at Silver Creek Preserve where they went

*Gretchen Fraser lines up for another race on Warm Springs in 1986
at 67 years of age.* LUANNE PFEIFER

ski run   PAGE 4 · SEPTEMBER 1986

America's 50th Ski Birthday Bash

SKI INNOVATORS, from left to right, Bob Lange, plastic ski boot; Howard Head, the metal ski; and Ed Scott, creator of the modern ski pole, being inducted into Ski Magazine's Business Hall of Fame by publisher George Bauer.

THE LEGENDARY 110 year old Herman Smith "Jack Rabbit" Johannsen with Stein Ericksen's 4 year old son, Bjorn.

Story used by permission of Ski Business Magazine

By Luanne Pfeifer

It was a week where being 50 was the most glamorous age to be — especially for the ski world. From all over the world came the legendary people of skiing to this Idaho valley bright with sunshine and newly-fallen snow from Feb. 1₋7.

Famous Names Celebrate

Flocking to the dazzling double 50th birthday party for Sun Valley Ski Resort and *Ski* Magazine were the ski innovators, Olympians, movie celebrities, ski area builders, the sport's manufacturers and retailers, and countless aficionados of the sport of skiing.

Lights and ice sculptures on the one-mile entrance road leading to the Idaho resort set the pace for arriving dignitaries coming into the new-snow covered valley that Averill Harriman caused to be built in 1936 as "the site of a novel destination ski resort — a first in the United States — to rival any resort found in Europe."

spills, and excitement of the sport, and contributed to its growth.

Governor Evans stayed throughout the week of festivities, declaring Wednesday, Feb. 5 Warren Miller day. The California ski movie maker was presented with a plaque for his part in making tourism Idaho's third most important industry.

Scotty Toasted and Roasted

Idaho's governor John Evans turned out on crutches (from jogging, not skiing!) to honor the hometown Ketchum boy, Ed Scott, who turned ski poles to gold. Scott, characterized as a "Deep Freeze Don Quixote," was inducted into the Ski Business Hall of Fame, a prestigious group of innovators who changed the sport of skiing.

In accepting the award from former Olympian and ski coach, Chuck Ferries, Scott recalled how the first time he ever skied was without poles.

"Now poles are essential. Even the Pope is a Pole," quipped Scotty.

Racing Through the Decades

American skiing's 50th party brought together not only the leaders and the legends of the ski industry but also the equipment and apparel which

across the finish line, trying to maintain balance on wooden skis with no edges, she ended up in the arms of Bauer, who had raced down the widegate course just before her.

For the decade of the '50s, Fred Merchant of Gates Gloves, captured the costume title in the "embryo" Marker release bindings made famous by the "Marker Out" ads. Tom Shanklin was the fastest of the '50s era men on 1957 Rossignol slalom skis. Former Olympian and ski retailer, Sally Neidlinger Hudson, posted the fastest women's time wearing the same sweater that she wore when she won the U.S. National women's slalom race at Sun Valley in 1951, a title that put her on the 1952 Olympic team.

Other skiing immortals and equipment which was hot in its day were: Tom Corcoran, fourth in 1960 Olympics, on classic Rossignol Stratos 102; John Fry, *Ski* Magazine, on Head 360s, circa 1965; and Seth Masia, Ski Magazine's equipment editor, using reverse shoulder technique with Rossignol Strato skis loaned him by Olympic silver medalist Billy Kidd. · · · ·

Overall Best Costume · · · ·

for a few nights at a time, staying in an old cabin at Stalker Creek Ranch, to watch the ducks and geese in flight. They were fascinated by their beauty in formation against the purple and brown velvet mountains of southern Idaho. This last remnant of Idaho's frontier—silver water, green cottonwoods and a kaleidoscope sky at sunset—seemed to survive the ravages of time like the Frasers themselves.

Hikes, especially with friends such as Bill and Rosie Hewlett, were also a part of their summers. A collection of radiant wildflower photos taken by Don occupied a prominent place framed on the wall of their Elkhorn home.

ski run SEPTEMBER 1986 · PAGE 5

TIME CAPSULE ceremony at the base of Ruud Mt. The time capsule is to be opened in 50 years for Sun Valley and Ski Magazine's 100th Anniversary. Left to right, Chuck Webb, Sun Valley assistant general manager; Ginger Piotter, Sun Valley Ketchum Regional History department; Charlie Proctor, Sigmund Ruud's daughter; Kathleen Mortemer Harriman, Averell's daughter; Governor John Evans, state of Idaho; Carol and Earl Holding, owners of Sun Valley; and George Bauer, publisher of Ski Magazine.

Sun Valley's 50th

continued from previous page

were at Dollar Mountain and at the bottom of the Warm Spring's lifts with demo equipment.

By the fourth day of the celebration the parties got louder and a 20-hour snowstorm continued to fall. A time capsule was planted to be opened after the next 50 years and everyone vowed to be there when *that* party took place.

A Week of Reunions

"Skiing has experienced a 13 percent growth rate in the last 16 years which is two times the CNP," summed up Don Gogle, vice-president of Kidder, Peabody & Co., during one of Ski Magazine's Business Week sessions.

It was a week-long celebration of reunions from past ski encounters whether on the race course, the manufacturing ski world, or the 10th Moun...

counted war stories in The Lodge's new Gretchen's Restaurant (formerly Duchin Dining room) amidst memorabilia donated by Gretchen Fraser of Sun Valley, the racer who brought home America's first Olympic gold medal in skiing.

The Professional Ski Instructors of America graced the mountains with demonstrations of ski techniques through the ages. Long forgotten techniques such as Arlberg, Reverse Shoulder, wedelin all came back in deja vu for today's skiers to imitate.

Meanwhile, over on Sun Valley's Baldy Mountain, a 20-category NASTAR race took lace with gold, silver, and bronze medals awarded in various categories, such as ski manufacturers, media, area personnel, and ski retailers.

All too soon the closing fireworks lit up the night sky over Dollar Mountain. A giant 50 in flares blazed on the hillside above the...

"The '80s are great...but those were the days," summed up Christen Cooper.

In a glass case at the newly-remodeled Sun Valley Lodge lobby, Cooper's 1984 silver Olympic medal was displayed with Gretchen Fraser's gold medal won 36 years before. They represented the past and present for ski history.

The ordinary skiers, however, who came to celebrate represented the eternal flame of the sport. As Peter Duchin's band played, all joined in singing "Happy Birthday American Skiing." There was a lump in many a throat for the equipment, the techniques, and the ski areas had changed, but not the people.

In 1986 when Sun Valley hosted its own elegant 50th birthday party, Gretchen was honorary queen. She grandly showed up to walk under crossed ski poles into rooms crowded with long time skiers. Her Olympic gold medal hung around her neck and she wore the après ski skirt she took to the 1948 Olympics. (How many women could fit into the same skirt 38 years later?)

Few people knew it then, but only weeks before she had been diagnosed by her family doctor, Royal McClure, at Moritz Hospital to have angina. She needed heart surgery but she put it off until after the celebration because everyone was counting on her presence.

On February 25, 1986, after the 50th ski celebration was over she had quadruple bypass surgery. It was her second open-chest surgery.

Two years later, for their 49th wedding anniversary, the Frasers took an 8-day bicycle trip through Europe. Don was 75 years of age and Gretchen 69 but the vineyards plus Milan and Venice became a shorter rerun of Don's youth when he bicycled through Europe after the 1936 Olympics.

Gretchen had been fighting cancer for years. The sun had taken its toll on her light-hued Norwegian skin. In addition to the coronary bypass surgeries she underwent cancer surgery many times for melanoma, starting in the late 1960s.

She once said whenever she was a little disgusted with all her health problems she relieved the difficulty by thinking of others and doing something for someone else.[7]

"I think she spent three-quarters of her time helping others," said Bill Janss, a friend since early Harriman Cup days.

Only when her long-time medical problems come to light do people understand that her quietly rendered gifts of kindness, generosity and inspiration for others—the do-something-for-someone-else acts—were really her own unique way of dealing with her long-time health concerns.

All of the forementioned renditions of Gretchen's gifts, do not imply she was a saint recruited off a pedestal in Saint Peter's Square. With a bit of humor, as was her way, she could be heard to offer a quiet aside showing how much she disliked people unduly impressed with themselves.

As the years passed and new American ski champions took the podium, Gretchen Fraser's name almost vanished. Every four years when the Olympics were held a few reporters remembered she was still alive.

She was not idle, though. The one thing that caused her to complain was an article once written about her saying she was spending her time doing nothing.

Ex-Olympic star finds oblivion keeps her busy

By JIM POORE
The Idaho Statesman

SUN VALLEY — In 1948, they stopped a presidential cabinet meeting over her, squired her down Broadway in a New York City ticker tape parade and asked her to be on the front of the Wheaties box.

Gretchen
Fraser

In 1980, Gretchen Fraser, the first U.S. skier ever to win a gold medal in the Winter Olympics, has to chuckle over the way modern historians look at her career.

. "A ski magazine did a story on me," Fraser said, "and though I can't quote it exactly, it said something like, 'I won the first American ski medals, had a child and went back home to oblivion.' "

If oblivion includes logging 3,000 hours flying, running an aviation committee, serving 27 years on a hospital board, being on the U.S. Olympic equestrian committee, starting the first amputee skiing group, participating in numerous air shows and going to Europe six times as the guest of various skiing groups, then there might be a long line wanting to join her in oblivion, wherever that is these days.

The Frasers—they met when she was a teenager and the love affair lasted a lifetime. Together they were always young at-heart. This photo was taken about the time of their Golden Wedding Anniversary. KETCHUM-SUN VALLEY HISTORICAL MUSEUM COLLECTION

"A magazine did a story on me that said something like 'I won the first American ski medals, had a child, and went back home to oblivion.'" she complained.

Oblivion! If oblivion is logging 3,000 hours piloting airplanes; running an aviation committee; serving 27 years on a hospital board; being on the U.S. equestrian committee; starting one of the first amputee skiing groups; coaching the Idaho Special Olympics; going to Europe more than six times for various international ski fucntions plus all the foregoing Sun Valley episodes then the dictionary can rewrite the definition of the word, oblivion.

The rest of the world may have forgotten her. But in Sun Valley, she was always prominent among the locals. She walked among them and they remembered how she had countless times, not just in the Olympics, figured out a way to do what was difficult, if not impossible, and to never quit.

At her last Sun Valley Ski Club reunion in 1994 she was vibrant but frail. Her husband of 53 years had died of a heart attack a few weeks before. Their 50th Wedding Anniversary celebration had come and gone a few years previously. Don had lived more than 25 active years since being revived by electric shock treatment, after his first heart problem.

Warren Miller, whom the club was honoring that week, stopped his talk to introduce Gretchen to a packed-room audience after his wife, Laurie, prompted her film maker husband that she had just slipped in. The entire room stood up; to Sun Valley people she was ski royalty.

The next day she led a few friends on a cross country ski trek, sometimes breaking the trail, in an attempt to keep up her spirits. The First Lady of Ski Racing, at 75 years of age, was supposed to leave in a few weeks to receive a Founders of Skiing award in Santa Fe, New Mexico. Even at that stage in life she was still sometimes called upon to live up to the legend status, to receive another honor or to give back, by her presence, to the sport that which it had provided for her.

She never made it to Santa Fe. A week before she was to fly to New Mexico she was taken to the hospital with coronary arrest and no will to live. She pulled through and came home. Kathy Harriman Mortimer, her long-time friend, stayed with her until the home nurse took over. Then she left to return to New York. Within a few days Gretchen had another heart failure dying 36 days after Don. She always said she would stay alive to take care of Don and she did.

Mission accomplished.

In the Sun Valley Lodge five days later, a memorial service was held. Gretchen's grandchildren, Jeff and Heather, plus her son, Bill, and his wife, Linda, were there from Woodinville, Washington.[8]

The private green and white jet of Sun Valley's owner, Earl Holding, was suddenly on the runway of the little Hailey, Idaho airport. Holding had returned. It was surprising to residents because he had only recently left from Salt Lake City in his personal plane for the 1994 Olympics in Norway and the Games were still in progress.

Averell Fisk, a grandson of Sun Valley's founder was there to do a reading on behalf of Kathleen Mortimer. Averell Harriman's widow, the American Ambassador to France, sent a letter to be read on her behalf. A poem was read by Cameron Cooper for Glenn and Bill Janss.

Dead was the woman who had lived in the legends she helped each of the three owners of Sun Valley create for the mountains of Idaho.

EIGHT

Medals Ever After

THE TRAIL TO THE OLYMPIC victory podium or to a World Cup title is an intricate one. It is a pathway where parents, local ski clubs, volunteer officials and U.S. Skiing officials all join together to provide a support structure for aspiring U.S. Ski Team competitors. Could it be that a role model helps, acting as a catalyst, to make the Olympic torch burn brighter lighting the way more clearly for those who aspire to athletic excellence?

Is that why four women ski racers from one ski area alone returned home with Olympic medals? Or was it just coincidence in life's game of chance? Was there some link between Gretchen's gold and silver way back in 1948 and the other Sun Valley medalists who followed?

Such questions remained for me uppermost throughout the writing of this book. After Gretchen's silver and gold in 1948, the women of Sun Valley accumulated an impressive list for a single ski area: Susan Corrock, bronze medalist in downhill in 1972 Winter Olympics in Sapporo, Japan; Christin Cooper, silver medalist in giant slalom in the 1984 Winter Olympics in Sarajevo, Yugoslavia; and Picabo Street, silver medalist in downhill at the 1994 Winter Olympics in Lillehammer, Norway.

Were each of these competitors influenced through the years by Gretchen who lived so vitally and visibly involved among them at Sun Valley?

Each racer first knew about Gretchen from a parent. (Isn't that is how most legends start and are passed down through the generations). As each came to know Gretchen personally, since she was always active among the racers of Sun Valley, they picked up a different spark from the Olympic flame which she carried all through her life.

The racers, their coaches, and their parents told me of Gretchen and how she influenced their lives. The following are their stories:

Susan ("Susie") Corrock Luby

"If American skiing needed a road map to Olympic greatness it would have to be her (Gretchen Fraser)," said Susan Corrock Luby, 23 years after her Olympic bronze medal win. Reached in Spokane, Washington, where she lives as a busy mother of two grade school age children. She talked of hearing about Gretchen from her parents, Jack and Lila Corrock.

The Corrocks owned a hotel near the other side of the mountain from where Gretchen, many years before, had learned to ski. While living in Seattle, the Corrocks managed the Alpine Inn at Crystal Mountain a few miles outside the Sunrise (northern) entrance to Mount Rainier National Park. It was at Crystal Mountain and at Steven's Pass that the Corrock children learned to ski.

In 1970, when her parents moved to Sun Valley where they live today, Susie was by then already on the national team. So though Sun Valley became her home and place where she hung her skis, most of her pre-Olympic training was done in Colorado, where the U.S.Ski Team trained in the '70s. But she never forgot her roots in the shadow of Mount Rainier, the view-dominating mountain where Gretchen learned to ski.

Influenced by her parent's renditions of Gretchen, she always thought of her as "understated elegance." When the two

Sapporo, Japan, Feburary 4, 1972, Susan Corrock, Ketchum, Idaho, in action during Friday's dress rehearsal for the Women's Olympic Downhill race. If it had been the real thing she would have won with a time of 1:40.52. AP WIREPHOTO

Olympians finally did meet, Susie started telling Gretchen how hard the training was. The elder Olympian laughed telling of some of the long pre-race hikes up the mountains of Sun Valley in the early days. Susie was impressed with Gretchen's dedication and drive.

During the Legends Reunion of former Olympians at Stratton Mountain, years after both of their Olympic performances, the two medalists roomed together. They both recognized the influence of skiing parents as contributing factors to their Olympic wins. Susie saw Gretchen through the years whenever she returned there to ski and visit her parents. As she tells it, her parents provided for her a road map containing two familiar mountains where Gretchen had etched her name. She couldn't have had a better role model.

Christin ("Coop") Cooper Taché

Reached in Aspen, Colorado, where she lives with her pro ski racing husband, Mark Taché, the former Olympian had just returned from a 1995 humanitarian trip to Sarajevo where, 11 years earlier, she had won a silver medal for the U.S. and Sun Valley in Olympic giant slalom. She had just delivered her first "Spirit of HOPE" planeload of sporting equipment for the teens of Sarajevo.

Unlike her previous arrival in Sarajevo with the U.S. Olympic Ski Team, this time she arrived by military transport and was hurried into an armored personnel carrier headed for Dobrinja, the bombed-out Press Village of the Sarajevo Games.

Word of Sarajevo's war-torn plight had filtered to her. She had been moved to mobilize (starting with phone calls) former Olympians to help her provide a sports program for the war-devastated teens of the Olympic city that had been so gracious to all athletes in 1984.

"The Olympians needed to repay a debt," said Coop.

Then she campaigned passionately to the members of the Ski Industries America (SIA).

America's athletes and industry heard.

Because of the fighting going on there, she realized she could not get to Mount Jahorina, site of her silver medal victory. The Serb-held territory was where the mortar and artillery were fired from. She was, however, able to get to Dobrinja, one of the hardest hit and most isolated sections of the former Olympic city. So that was where her sporting equipment was distributed. Piles

Christin Cooper at 18, shown racing to victory in the U.S. Nationals at Sun Valley in 1977. SUN VALLEY NEWS BUREAU

of it had previously been unloaded on to the tarmacs of Split and Zegreb.

In front of the bombed out press building Sarajevo's teens started flying Frisbees . . . playing volleyball . . . kicking soccer balls. It was hard to tell who had the bigger smiles on their faces—Christin's crew or Sarajevo's teens, most of whom had lost, due to war, their brothers and fathers . . . and all hope of a pleasurable future.

Someone cared.

Broadcaster, Greg Lewis, co-founder of HOPE (Humanitarian Olympians for PEace) explained the mission thus:

"Let us remember that the essential message of the Games is not found in triple axles, slap shots or medal counts. It is found in 44 words of the Olympic Charter:

'The goal of the Olympic Movement is to contribute to building a peaceful and better world by educating youth through sport practiced without discrimination of any kind, and in the Olympic spirit, which requires mutual understanding with a spirit of friendship, solidarity and fair play,' "

Just as Gretchen had carried the torch beyond the gates of the Olympic Village to help handicapped skiers and mentally challenged children in her post-Olympic life, so Coop's spirit of HOPE became her way of paying back the Olympic experience.

Throughout her race training at Sun Valley Christin had known of Gretchen from her mother (Glenn Cooper Janss) and stepfather (Bill Janss). She was inspired by Gretchen's dedication to people other than just fine tuned athletes. She got to know Gretchen personally during the time Gretchen was involved with The Idaho Special Olympics for mentally challenged children.

When she was on the U.S. Ski Team, Coop often went to the Fraser's condo for tea between races whenever she returned to Sun Valley. The Frasers were living in a Villager condo and later a Snowcreek condo at the time, both within walking distance of the Lodge, prior to moving to their final home in

Christin Cooper, 1984 Olympic silver medalist, displays a trail sign named after her achievement. SUN VALLEY CO.

Elkhorn. Perhaps it was there that Christin began to assimi-late that after one wins a medal one learns, as Gretchen did, to carry the torch beyond the gates of the Olympic Village.

Christin saw and learned first hand of Gretchen's dignity, dedication, and compassion for others.

Later during her Spirit of HOPE campaign, Christin was to tell a reporter "My belief is athletes, if we want better role models, must begin to stand for more than our muscles and pocketbooks."[1]

About the time Coop started ski racing with her Sun Val-ley grade school classmates, her father, a prominent speed-boat hydrofoil racer, had just died in a Santa Monica hospital after a battle with cancer. Her widowed mother, Glenn Candy Cooper, moved to Sun Valley from Malibu, California and it was there Christin entered the national team by way of the race training program of the Sun Valley Ski Educational Foundation which Gretchen had helped found in 1960.

Michel Rudigoz, then with the Sun Valley Ski Educational Foundation, was her coach when she was 12 years old. He became a U.S. Ski Team coach for eight years, returning to Sun Valley in 1984, the same year Christin won her silver. When he returned to coaching for the Sun Valley Ski Educational Foun-dation he quickly spotted another woman racer, also 12 years old at the time, who was destined for Olympic greatness. That second racer was Picabo Street.

In the '90s Christin is quick to explain that Picabo's great gliding ability, so necessary in downhill racing, was acquired on the numerous cat tracks of Sun Valley where the racing team periodically lets loose.

If you ask Michel what Sun Valley has that produces the Olympic medalists he will tell you, "It is the nature of the mountain. It has no flat places. It's downhill all the way so one never poles there as one would while skiing many of the runs at other resorts."

If you ask Christin about the terrain at Sun Valley she will tell you the mountain (meaning Bald Mountain or "Baldy") is the greatest coach. But it is also the way the village of Sun Valley has a tradition of racing which gives competitors such an edge.

"Everyone from the person who pumps gas to the waiters in restaurants all treat the racers with respect. I don't see that in other U.S. ski areas. Only in Europe does one find the same aura," says Christin.

When Christin left for her first Olympic competition in 1980 at Lake Placid, Gretchen gave her the Ullr medallion she had carried all through her racing days. Ullr, the Norse god of skiers, Gretchen said would bring good luck to its wearer. She wanted Christin to have it.

When, in 1982, Christin won three medals in the World Championships the Frasers gave her a piece of jewelry depicting the Sun Valley sun in gold. Again in 1984 when Christin won the Olympic silver medal another jewelry piece was fashioned by Tom Keenan of Towne & Parke jewelers of Sun Valley as a gift from the Frasers. It was an early race medallion of Gretchen's surrounded by a bezel of diamonds.

(To me it was the Frasers way of carrying on—with a touch of class—the elegance of Averell Harriman who, in 1948, bestowed on her the gift of a Tiffany gold 4-leaf clover pin. See Chapters V when Gretchen was given it and Chapter VII when she found someone else, Muffy Davis, who needed the boost in their life that the Tiffany piece had provided her in 1948.)

The year before the XIVth Winter Olympics in Sarajevo, "Coop" had a broken bone under the knee and a piece of bone was grafted from the hip to raise the compression fracture. During the Games she was 24 years old and had been eight years on the U.S. Ski Team. She was out for gold. Someone once said: She did not lose the gold; she won the silver. For anyone else it would have been a setback but for Christin she answered reporters questions by saying, "You can take the joy out of life by wanting something better all the time."

Life sits softly on Coop's shoulders. She articulated her situation so well she was drafted to become a television commentator for CBS the following Olympics. Bill Marolt, U.S. Alpine director 1978 to 1984 and U.S. Skiing's CEO in 1996, said of her, "She is tough as nails on the hill but off she's a lady."

Throughout Coop's racing career, Don and Gretchen exchanged letters with her. So, of course, Gretchen easily influenced her.

With free lance writing and TV commentaries and her latest humanitarian efforts for the children of Sarajevo, Cooper has proved that all Olympians can be a powerful resource for good on a global scale.

Like Gretchen she did not pack up her medals and go home.

Picabo ("Skeek") Street

Picabo Street, America's first ever World Champion downhiller, World Cup downhill winner and a silver medalist in the Lillehammer Olympics of 1994, always referred to Gretchen as a "Pillar of Courage." She was talking about Gretchen's long time battle with cancer. In the language of Picabo, Gretchen was a "straight source" of someone in turmoil who carried on.

Picabo's mother, Dee Street, had a good friend who was battling cancer and lost. That greatly affected both mother and daughter.

Picabo—with almost a 50 year age span between herself and Gretchen—only knew Gretchen in her later years. She saw the elder racer as someone who had things stacked up against her, with the cancer and two heart bypass surgeries (comprising six grafts), but carried on. Because the Streets had the same doctor as Gretchen in the Wood River Valley, Picabo knew of the health battles Gretchen faced. She admired her spunk.

In 1968 Hannah Locke Carter's youngest daughter, Ann, was working at a restaurant in Sun Valley with Picabo's dad.

Picabo—" a gift from heaven," said FIS president Marc Holder. Circa 1994. SUN VALLEY CO.

Ann's mother, was an early Sun Valley racer (see Chapter II) invited by Averell Harriman to train in Sun Valley. Through Hannah's daughter, Ann, Picabo met Kathleen Harriman Mortimer, resulting in eventually meeting Gretchen. Though the age spread was epic, the two competitors shared ski racing stories.

"What better company to be in than in Sun Valley where people win medals and know how to wear them," said Dee Street in the summer of 1995 after her daughter won the World Cup downhill title. She had lived in the Wood River Valley for 30 years and watched the athletes. Her daughter was shown an example in Gretchen that a person does not load up their medals and go home to gloat. They keep on going and go on throughout life.

The tie to Gretchen was so great that parents and coaches decided not to tell Picabo of Gretchen Fraser's death which occurred February 17, 1994, two days before Picabo was to race the downhill in which she received her Olympic silver medal.

After the downhill, in an attempt to link the two Sun Valley racers, the media reported that Gretchen had given something to Picabo before the Olympics. Gretchen did not do this as she was pre-occupied just before the Games opened with the death of her husband of 53 years.

Despite what the press, television, coaches and public relations people say, Gretchen never gave any good luck gift to Picabo. It would have been characteristic of Gretchen to do so but she never did. Yet everything, from the #1 racing bib of the '48 Olympics to a diamond pin, was erroneously reported to have been given to Picabo by Gretchen. It would have made a poignant tie-in story, but that never happened. Dee Street who was there confirms this, saying she does not know how that rumor started.

The Streets arrived in Lillehammer the night before Picabo's silver medal win in the downhill. They stayed at

American ski promoter, Bernie Weichsel's, house which he had rented in Norway.

"I hoped for a win but did not rehearse it," said Picabo's mother. She didn't want to jinx it. She simply gave Picabo posters from all the ski shops in the Wood River Valley. The family didn't sleep that night, talking after the draw (allocation of bib numbers). Truth is: they didn't sleep for three days.

When Picabo wearing her Olympic silver medal, arrived back in Sun Valley after the Lillehammer Games, a celebration party was held on the Lodge terrace.

There Wallace Huffman, general manager of Sun Valley, summed up the winter of 1994 by saying:

"It was a year of giving and taking."

In the space of two days that year Sun Valley had lost their icon, named Gretchen, but gained a new light, named Picabo.

After the celebration one of the local kids came up to Picabo and said, "I want to be a champion like you. What do I have to do?" (It was a question young racers had often asked of Gretchen but she was no longer there. The torch had **now** been passed on to another).

Street already knew what her answer would be: "I'd tell him or her to go free ski . Even if you miss training gates its beneficial to free ski. You have to know how to turn."[2] Life is reduced to basics with Picabo.

A year after the celebration, in the summer of 1995 in Budapest, Hungary, when Salt Lake City was bidding for the Winter Olympics to be held in the year 2002, Picabo—as part of the American delegation—was welcomed by Marc Hodler, president of the Federation of International Skiing. He cited her as an incident in the ski world, quickly adding, "She's not an incident. She is a gift from Heaven."

Then Picabo turned on her high voltage smile, talked freely to delegates in Picabo language . . . and America was awarded the Winter Olympics for the year 2002.[3]

Before the new-millennium Games, however, there is one more Olympics to close the 1900s. The 1998 Winter Games in Nagano, Japan, closes this book (and also this Olympic century) as it is the last Olympics of the 1900s. Ironically it marks the 50th year celebration since America received its first Olympic gold medal in skiing, via Gretchen Fraser. Times and racing have changed but not the Olympic spirit. It still blazes brightly in America though the original torch bearer no longer can be seen on the streets, pathways and trails of Sun Valley.

Gretchen Claudia Fraser (1919–1994) is not alive now. May the stories of her life and her true Olympian spirit live on to inspire others into the far future.

Like footprints in new fallen snow she left a mark but nary a stain.

N O T E S

Chapter I (pages 3–24)

[1] Don Fraser oral history tape, 1986, Regional History Department, Ketchum Community Library, Ketchum, Idaho.

[2] Pfeifer, Luanne "Sun Valley Salad Days," *West Magazine, Los Angeles Times,* Sunday December 8, 1969, (Averell Harriman interview by Luanne Pfeifer)

[3] Lang, Otto, *Bird of Passage:* Helena, Montana, Falcon Press, 1994.

Chapter II (pages 25–42)

[1] Nevin, David, *The Moon is a Balloon:* New York, Putnam, 1972.

[2] Gretchen Fraser oral history tape, Regional History Department, Ketchum Community Library, Ketchum, Idaho, 1986.

[3] Jerome, John, *The Man on the Medal*, copyright Richard and Margaret Durrance, Durrance Enterprises, PO Box 6396, Snowmass Village, Colorado 81615. In a longer version of this race in this book, Dick was shouting, "Too fast," in both German and English.

[4] Sun Valley Ski Club Annual, 1940.

[5] Gretchen Fraser, oral history tape, Regional History Department, Ketchum Community Library, 1986.

[6] Robertson, Patrick, *Guinnes Film Facts and Feats,* 1985.
The first golden disc awarded for a record selling over 1 million copies was presented to bandleader Glenn Miller on 10 February 1942 for "Chattanooga Choo Choo," the hit song he and his orchestra performed in the movie "Sun Valley Serenade."

[7] *Newsweek,* June, 1992.

[8] Marshall, Jamie, editor, *The Aspens, a Guide Book,* Aspen Skiing Co., 1989.

[9] Lund, Morten and Pfeifer, Friedl, *Nice Going,* Pictorial Histories Publishing Co., Missoula, MT, 1993.

Chapter III (pages 43-50)

[1] Taylor, Dorice *Sun Valley:* Sun Valley, Idaho: Ex Libris Books, 1980.

Chapter IV (pages 51–88)

[1] Gretchen Fraser oral history tape, 1986, Regional History Department of the Ketchum Community Library

[2] American Ski Annual, 1948.

[3] Chadwick, Gloria, *A History of the United States Ski Association*, Colorado Springs: U.S. Ski Association, 1962.

[4] Schroeder, William R., *The Story of the Winter Olympic Games* The Helms Athletic Foundation, Los Angeles, 1960.

[5] Gretchen kept a diary for the dates she was away for the Olympic Games. The entries used in this chapter are thus her own words and thoughts on events. The clipped sentences reflect the small amount of time she had to make the entries.

[6] Gretchen Fraser oral history tape 1984, Regional History Dept., Ketchum Community Library. Also David Butterfield video, Ketchum-Sun Valley Ski & Heritage Museum

[7] Poole, Jim, February, 1981 interview of Gretchen Fraser for *The Idaho Statesman*

[8] Fraser, Gretchen, "I Found I was Good Enough to Win" *"Ski Magazine*, February 1960.

[9] Gretchen Fraser oral history, 1984, Regional History Department, Ketchum Community Library. All the racers including Averell Harriman's daughter, Kathleen, called him Ave. So the reference to W. Averell Harriman as "Ave" in this book is not intended to diminish the stature of the famous diplomat who served in high posts for five U.S. presidents and preferred most people outside ski circles to call him Governor. (His term as governor of New York (1958–59) was won by public election, all other offices were appointive) He died July 26, 1986, at age 94.

[10] Laughlin, James, "The 1948 Olympics" *American Ski Annual*, 1948.

[11] Barber, Red, "Red Barber Memories", *Christian Science Monitor*, February 26, 1988.

[12] Pfeifer, Luanne, "Sun Valley Salad Days, *West Magazine* of the *Los Angeles Times*, , December 8, 1969 (interview with W. Averell Harriman by Luanne Pfeifer)

Chapter V (pages 89–100)

[1] There is some mix-up as to Gretchen doing stand-in skiing for Margaret Sullavan. For a movie called "The Immortal Storm," which was never released, she did some skiing scenes for Margaret Sullavan dressed in a skirt and flesh colored tights. MGM later released the movie as "The Mortal Storm." Gretchen was supposed to ski for Margaret Sullavan in the remake but by then she was recuperating from a ski injury so she got Beth Crookes to do the stand-in ski scenes. Beth

158

was the wife of Darroch Crookes who was a member of the 1936 Men's Olympic Team with Don Fraser. The two men worked for the Union Pacific Railroad about this time. Don in Sun Valley and Darroch Crookes in Portland.

After the war the two men became business partners in Don's petroleum products distributorship in the Portland-Vancouver area.

[2] A secretary for Sun Valley Resorts, sent Gretchen all the U.P. correspondence in a file marked with her name on it. This was correspondence between Union Pacific in Omaha, Nebraska and Sun Valley, Idaho. In this chapter the endorsement facts were assembled from that file.

The letter read:

June 29, 1977

Dear Mrs Fraser:

We have recently run across several older files in our Administration area of the offices. I am enclosing your personal file for the years 1948 to 1953. I hope it brings back many smiles and memories to you.
Sincerely,
Sun Valley Resorts, Inc.
Candace Anderson, Secretary to Rene L. Meyer

Gretchen saved the large assembly of letters (hers handwritten and UP's typewritten) which proved valuable in the documenting of the facts for this chapter.

The Barsis drawing presented to her was by Max Barsis a former law student from Austria who came to Sun Valley. In Austria he did not want to go into law practice and so he used to spend his time in court drawing sketches of the witnesses. When he came to the United States he took up cartooning in Sun Valley. The Union Pacific Railroad hired him to draw sketches of the guests on the deck at Round House restaurant. Two books of his ski cartoons were published in the 1940s.

Chapter VI (page 101–112)

[1] Steve Hannegan Associates prepared a report giving photos and documentation of the promotional trip in 1950. The statistics in this chapter were taken from that bound documentation prepared by the public relations firm for the Union Pacific Railroad.

[2] Newberger, Richard and Maurine, "Ski Whiz" an interview of Gretchen Fraser for *Liberty Magazine* , 1949.

[3] Odmark, Leif, interview by Luanne Pfeifer, February 1996. He was at the meeting since he was men's coach of the 1952 U.S. cross country team.

[4] The U.S. Ski Team has a full-time academic and career counselor interfacing, since the 1980s, with schools and academies to keep young athletes moving education-wise while they disrupt their normal classes to train and compete. One important academic standard: athletes must complete high school with diploma by their 19th birthday or face sanctions limiting them from U.S. Ski Team activities and funding.

Chapter VII (page 113–142)

[1] Poole, Jim, February, 1980 interview of Gretchen Fraser for *The Idaho Statesman*

[2] Fraser, Don, letter to Lowell Thomas, August 14, 1980, Sun Valley Idaho.

[3] Pfeifer, Luanne, February, 1998 interview and letter enclosing clips from Gene Nora Jessen, past president of the Idaho Ninety Nines.

[4] Davis, Muffy, Letters to the Editor, *Wood River Journal*, February 1994.

[5] Pfeifer, Luanne interview of W. Averell Harriman for *West Magazine* of the *Los Angeles Times*, December 8, 1969.

[6] Pfeifer, Luanne "Bugsy: The Rest of the Story," *Snowcountry* magazine, October, 1992.

[7] Gretchen Fraser answers written questions to the Idaho Girl Scouts, November, 1975.

[8] According to Bill Fraser (their son), the Fraser's black Labrador dog named Annie sat in the front row with him. It was the only time the Lodge made the concession to (knowingly) let a dog into the interior of the Lodge. Sun Valley Co. permitted this in deference to Gretchen. The room was packed and I never saw the dog.

Chapter VIII (pages 143–156)

[1] Robbins, Paul "Return to Sarajevo" *U.S. Ski Team Magazine*, 1994.

[2] Press conference Sun Valley, Idaho, March, 1994 and *Wood River Journal* December 27, 1995.

[3] In the translation dictionary of the language of Picabo Street words like "fuck" and "kick-butt" appear. Whether the words remain into the new-millennium is a dilemma Picabo, the press and television face.

ACKNOWLEDGMENTS

MANY PEOPLE contributed to this book. Their names are inscribed in my heart. They are Patricia Butterfield, Jaci Wilkins, Sandy Hofferberg who are keepers of the great history of Sun Valley. The first two work in the Ketchum-Sun Valley Ski and Heritage Museum and the latter in the Regional History Department of the Ketchum Community Library. Their warm facilities and friendship to pursue the news clippings, tapes and videos of Gretchen's fête is immeasurable. I couldn't have done all the research it took without them.

Everyone who knew Gretchen offered tidbits and perception. I am indebted to Anita "Nitz" Gray, Hannah Carter, Kathleen Harriman Mortimer, Shirley Brashears, Leif Odmark, Walter Page, Phyllis Rice, Muffy Davis, Christin Cooper, Susie Corrock, Gene Nora Jesson, Gary Swartz, Bill Carson, Jack Sibbich, Lila Rosen, Barbara Hobbs, Wolfgang Lert, Peter Katz, Erica Spiess-Mehringer, Andrea Van Every (translator), Tom Keenan, Sandy Poulsen, Ruth Jones, Michel Rudigoz, Dee Street and Donald W. Fraser, Jr. Then there are also those who raced with Gretchen who set the stage: Dave Faires, Boots Blatt, Miggs Durrance and Bill Janss. Moreover, John Jay, who was official cinematographer at the 1948 Winter Olympics, spliced out a segment of Gretchen's win, put it on video and kindly projected it for me and others while I was writing the book.

I am indebted to Doug Pfeiffer who is supposed to be retired, after 15 years as Editor-in-chief for *Skiing Magazine*. He was consummate in his passion for the historical accuracy and his encouragement. With his great love for the technicalities of the

161

sport, i.e.: the ski equipment and the ski techniques through the years, he spent countless hours in polishing my words. To him it was fun—like skiing has always been to him. I value his expertise and his friendship.

Certain events and people came out of the blue. American FIS official, Gus Raaum, was taking his granddaughters on a trip to Norway and so I got the opening chapter's photograph of Gretchen's mother's home town taken by young Allison Raaum. Wolfgang Lert and Miggs Durrance skied with me at Aspen and gave some insight. As I had been a ski writer through three owners of the Sun Valley Resort, numerous public relations photos and events were already in my files where I had saved them through the years because my first memorable personality interview was with W. Averell Harriman for the *L.A. Times.*

Thanks also go to Kitty Herrin of Arrow Graphics for book design and composition and Stan Cohen of Pictorial Histories for publication assistance.

I was honored to have Bill Janss accept my request to do the Foreword and Bobby Burns of Sun Valley, a designer *extraordinaire*, do the book jacket cover design. Both are still skiing and deeply entrenched in Sun Valley. It kept everything in one family—the family of legends and lore Sun Valley has created through the years.

Luanne Pfeifer
Malibu, California
1996

Appendix

Gretchen Fraser circa 1947.

The Harriman Cup

SOME OF THE GREAT NAMES in alpine ski racing history competed in Sun Valley's Harriman Cup, named after the Union
Pacific's chairman of the board, W. Averell Harriman. A list of
the Cup winners of this yearly international race during the
time Sun Valley was owned by the Union Pacific Railroad is
presented here. This prominent early-day race is no longer held.

YEAR	DOWNHILL	SLALOM	COMBINED
1937	Dick Durrance	Dick Durrance	Dick Durrance
1938	Ulli Beutter	Walter Prager	Dick Durrance
	Grace Lindley	Grace Lindley	Grace Lindley
1939	Toni Matt	Friedl Pfeifer	Peter Radacher
	Erna Steuri	Erna Steuri	Erna Steuri
1940	Dick Durrance	Friedl Pfeifer	Dick Durrance
	Grace Lindley	Nancy R. Cooke	Marilyn Shaw
1941	Sigi Engl	Friedl Pfeifer	Friedl Pfeifer
	Gretchen Fraser	Nancy R. Cooke	Gretchen Fraser
1942	Barney McLean	Gordon Wren	Barney McLean
	Catherine Henck	Clarita Heath	Clarita Heath
1943–46	*No Harriman Cup races due to war years*		
1947	Edi Rominger	Barney McLean	Edi Rominger
	Georgette Thiolière	G. Thiolière	G. Thiolière
1948	Jack Reddish	Jack Reddish	Jack Reddish
	Janette Burr	Ann Win	Suzanne Harris
1949	Henri Oreiller	Henri Oreiller	Henri Oreiller
	L. Couttet-Schmitt	L. Couttet-Schmitt	L. Couttet-Schmitt
1950	Hans Nogler	Francois Baud	Hans Nogler
	Andrea Mead	Andrea Mead	Andrea Mead
1951	Verne Goodwin	Jack Reddish	Ernie McCulloch
	Rhoda Wurtele Eaves	Sandra Tomlinson	Rhoda W. Eaves
1952	Ernie McCulloch	Otto von Allmen	Ernie McCulloch
		& Hans Nogler	
	Rhona Gillis	Mary Jane Marin	Lois Woodworth

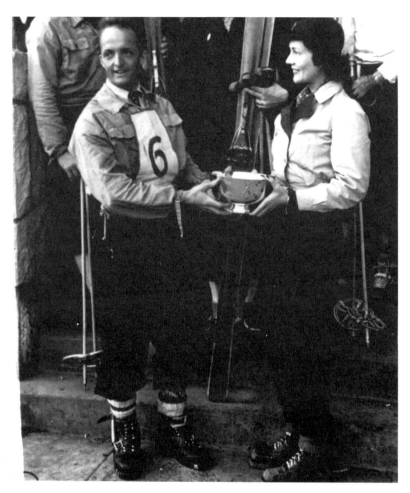

Dick Durrance receives the first Harriman Cup trophy from Mrs. Marie Harriman, 1937.

1953	Christian Pravda	Stein Ericksen	Christian Pravda
	Andrea Mead Lawrence	Sally Neidlinger	Andrea M. Lawrence
1954	Jack Reddish	Tom Corcoran	Tom Corcoran
	Janette Burr	Janette Burr	Janette Burr
1955	Martin Strolz	Martin Julen	Andrel Molterer
	Madeleine Berthod	Thea Hechleitner	M. Berthod
1956	Christian Pravda	Christian Pravda	Christian Pravda
	Sally Deaver	Sally Deaver	Sally Deaver
1957	Toni Sailer	Toni Sailer	Toni Sailer
	Freida Dancer	Inger Bjornbakken	Terese le Duc

1959	Christian Pravda	Christian Pravda	Christian Pravda
	Putzi Frandl	Linda Meyers	Putzi Frandl
1960	Willy Ferrer	Mathias Leitner	Adrien Duvillard
	Putzi Frandl	Traudl Hecker	Marianne Jahn
1961	Bud Werner	Billy Kidd	Jimmie Heuga
	Barbara Ferries	Barbara Ferries	Barbara Ferries
1963	Bud Werner	Bud Werner	Bud Werner
	Jean Saubert	Jean Saubert	Jean Saubert
	(SPECIAL GIANT SLALOM — Jos Minsch and Barbi Henneberger)		
1965	Karl Schranz	Michel Arpin	Karl Schranz
	Marielle Goitschel	Marielle Goitschel	Marielle Goitschel

NOTE: Dick Durrance and Christian Pravda are the only racers to retire the Harriman Cup, having won it three times.

Dick Durrance and W. Averell Harriman (rt) at a banquet when Durrance retired the Cup after winning it three times.

Karl Schranz at the Harriman Cup 1965. This was the first time in the U.S. an international downhill racer was seen wearing a one-piece skin-tight racing suit.

N.W. SKI CHAMPIONSHIP RESULTS
MEN'S DOWNHILL RACE

1. Don Fraser, Washington Ski club, 2:56.2; 2. John Woodward, Penguin Ski club, 3:05.4; 3. Lon Robinson, University of Washington, 3:08.4; 4. Harold Smith, Penguin Ski club, 3:09.3; 5. Arnt Ofstad, Spokane Ski club, 3:13.2; 6. Scott Osborn, Penguin Ski club, 3:15.3; 7. Paul Gilbreath, Washington Ski club, 3:17; 8. Darroch Crookes, Washington Ski club, 3:18.2; 9. Robert Higman, University of Washington, 3:22.1; 10. Boyd French Jr., Cascade Ski club, 3:23; 11. Henry Seidelhuber, Penguin Ski club, 3:27; 12. Olaf Rotegaard, Cascade Ski club, 3:28.1; 13. Kjell Kvale, Seattle Ski club, 3:29.2; 14. Hjalmar Hvam, Cascade Ski club, 3:33.3; 15. Jim Babson, Multnomah Athletic club, 3:33.4; 16. Ragnar Qvale, University of Washington, 3:38.4; 17. Ed Link, Sahalie Ski club, 3:41.4; 18. Art Granstrom, Wandermere Ski club, 3:42.4; 19. Bill Weir, Yakima Ski club, 3:51.3; 20. Al Boge, Spokane Ski club, 4:02; 21. Keith Whiting, Idaho Ski club, 4:03.4; 22. Fred Carter, Multonomah Athletic club, 4:10.4; 23. Vincent Broze, Seattle Ski club, 4:14; 24. Dave Nichols, Spokane Ski club, 4:20; 25. Rod Mackintosh, Yakima Ski club, 4:27.4; 26. Bob Isaacson, Spokane Ski club, 4:30.4; 27. Emil Cahen, Seattle Ski club, 4:36.3; 28. Mark Stephens, Yakima Ski club, 4:37.4; 29. Don Amick, Washington Ski club, 5:04.4; 30. John Ring, Spokane Ski club, 13:46 (lost in fog and snowstorm; was last starter).

Failed to finish: Hans Grage, Washington Ski club; Heige Sather, Leavenworth Ski club.

MEN'S COMBINED

	Downhill	Slalom	Total
1. Don Fraser	176.4	107.4	283.8
2. John Woodward	185.8	113.2	299.0
3. Lon Robinson	188.8	111.8	300.6
4. Harold Smith	189.6	122.2	311.8
5. Darroch Crookes	198.4	118.2	316.6
6. Paul Gilbreath	197.0	122.4	319.4
7. Boyd French Jr.	203.0	118.6	321.6
8. Scott Osborn	195.6	129.0	324.6
9. Henry Seidelhuber	207.0	117.6	324.6
10. Bob Higman	202.2	124.4	326.6
11. Kjell Qvale	209.4	120.8	330.2
12. Hjalmar Hvam	213.6	117.6	331.2
13. Arnt Ofstad	193.4	140.4	333.8
14. Jim Babson	213.8	137.2	351.0
15. Ragnar Qvale	218.4	136.4	354.8
16. Vincent Broze	254.0	125.8	379.8
17. Don Amick	304.4	107.0	411.4

WOMEN'S SLALOM

	1st Run	2nd Run	Total
1. Mrs. Skit S. Babson, Mult. A.C.	1:17.0	1:17.0	2:34.0
2. Gretchen Kunigk, Washington S.C.	1:22.0	1:19.1	2:41.2
3. Virginia Bowden, Washington S.C.	1:25.3	1:18.1	2:43.8
4. Ellis-Ayr Smith, Mult. A.C.	1:32.0	1:29.3	3:01.6
5. Betty Meachem, Washington A.C.	1:34.4	1:41.2	3:16.2
6. Mrs. Ada Darr, Mult. A.C.	1:48.1	1:47.3	3:55.8
7. Maryann Hill, Cascade S.C.	1:54.0	1:52.3	3:46.6

WOMEN'S COMBINED

	Downhill	Slalom	Total
1. Gretchen Kunigk	108.0	161.1	107.6
2. Mrs. Skit Smith Babson	141.0	154.0	118.0
3. Virginia Bowden	131.4	163.4	118.4
4. Betty Meacham	124.4	196.1	128.4
5. Ellis-Ayr Smith	140.4	181.3	128.8

Results of the Sugar Bowl Silver Belt Race

April 21, 1940

REISEN SLALOM FOR MEN

1. Friedl Pfeifer, Sun Valley	1.33.4
2. Dick Durrance, Sun Valley	1.35.0
3. Bili Pedlin, Washington S. C.	1.44.6
4. Sigfried Engl, Sun Valley	1.44.7
5. Richard Werle, Sun Valley	1.46.4
6. Fred Iselin, Sun Valley	1.48.8
7. John Blatt, Yosemite	1.53.0
8. Joe Ward, Woodstock S.C.	1.59.0
9. Henry Simmoneau, Mt. Mansfield	2.01.0
10. Toni Walsh, Sun Valley (Single Penalty)	2.03.0

SUGAR BOWL SILVER BELT RACE SLALOM FOR WOMEN

1. Gretchen Fraser, Sun Valley	1.14.0
2. Nancy Reynolds, Sun Valley	1.17.0
3. Lisl Durrance, Sun Valley	1.17.0
4. Margaret Jennings, Sugar Bowl	1.20.0
5. Shirley McDonald, Washington S.C.	1.26.0
6. Maryanne Hill, Cascade Ski Club	1.31.0
7. Dorothy Backus, Sugar Bowl SKi Club	1.38.0
8. Peggy Taylor, Sierra C.	1.56.0
9. Clarita Heath, Sun Valley	1.57.0
10. Betty Serugham, Reno S.C.	1.57.0

The 1948 Olympic Ski Team

WOMEN

Gretchen Fraser
Rebecca Fraser *(Cremer)*
Brynhild Grasmoen
Paula Kann *(Valar)*
Andrea Mead *(Lawrence)*
Dorthy Post *(Gann)*
Ruth-Marie Stewart *(Radamacher)*
Ann Winn

Susie Harris *(Rytting)* was selected as an alternate but stayed home.

The women are listed under their 1948 competition name. The name in parenthesis is their later married name.

MEN

Don Amick—A
John "Boots" Blatt— A
Robert Blatt— A
Wendall Broomhall—XC
Corey Engen— XC
David Faires—A
Sverre Fredheim—J
Devereaux Jennings— A
Donald Johnson—XC
Stephen Knowlton— A
Robert McLean—A
Richard Movitz—A
Paul Perrault—J
Jack Reddish—A
Colin Stewart—A
Ralph Townsend —XC
Gordon Wren —XC, J

Gretchen Fraser Race Results

1936–37

Novice Cup Award—based on 5 slalom races for novice skiers set on the lower end of Alta Vista Ridge, Mount Rainier *(her first race trophy)*
2nd Downhill—Cascade Ski Club Championships, Mount Hood
2nd Combined—Cascade Ski Club Championships, Mount Hood
1st Combined—Pacific Northwest Championships, Mount Spokane

1937-1938

1st—PNW Dowhill, Mount Hood
2nd—PNW Slalom, Mount Hood
1st—PNW combined, Mount Hood
1st—open slalom, Mt. Ranier
3rd—Harriman Cup downhill, Sun Valley
2nd—Harriman Cup combined, Sun Valley
1st—Silver Skis, Mount Rainier
1st—Golden Rose downhill, Mount Hood

1938-1939

10th—Northwest Ski Championships, Mount Hood
(Due to injuries sustained in the above Golden Rose downhill in June, 1938, this Championship in April, 1939 was the only race entered all season)

1939-40

1st—PNSA Championships, Yakima
1st—Jeffers Cup, Sun Valley
1st—Alta Snow Cup, Alta, Utah
4th combined—Harriman Cup, Sun Valley
Diamond Sun—*(award for timed run, top to bottom, on Baldy Mt., Sun Valley. Gretchen was one of the first women to receive it)*
1st—Silver Belt, Sugar Bowl, CA

1940–41

1st downhill—U.S. Nationals, Aspen, CO
3rd slalom—U.S. Nationals, Aspen, CO
1st combined—U.S. Nationals, Aspen, CO

1st downhill—Harriman Cup, Sun Valley
2nd slalom—Harriman Cup, Sun Valley
1st combined—Harriman Cup, Sun Valley

1941–42

1st slalom—The U.S. Nationals, Yosemite, CA
5th downhill—The U.S. Nationals, Yosemite, CA
1st—Snow Cup, Alta, Utah
1st—Jeffers Cup, Sun Valley
2nd combined—Harriman Cup, Sun Valley

1942–45 *No races due to World War II*

1945–46

1st—Portland Junior Chamber of Commerce Giant Slalom, Mount Hood
1st—Golden Rose Downhill, Mount Hood
(only two races entered due to bookkeeping duties of family business)

1946–47

1st downhill—PNSA Amateur Championships, Stevens Pass, WA
3rd slalom—PNSA Amateur Championships, Stevens Pass, WA
2nd combined—PNSA Amateur Championships, Stevens Pass, WA
1st downhill, slalom and combined—PNSA Open Championships,
   Mount Hood
1st downhill—Olympic Tryouts, Sun Valley
2nd slalom—Olympic Tryouts, Sun Valley
1st combined—Olympic Tryouts, Sun Valley
3rd downhill—Harriman Cup, Sun Valley
3rd slalom—Harriman Cup, Sun Valley
2nd combined—Harriman Cup, Sun Valley
1st—Golden Rose, Mount Hood

1947–48

Silver medal for combined—Vth Winter Olympic Games,
   St. Moritz, Switzerland
Gold medal in special slalom—Vth Winter Olympic Games,
   St. Moritz, Switzerland
*(Gretchen did not race in the U.S. this season because the entire team
left by ship December 8 for the Winter Olympics.)*